Entrepreneur Awakening:

Making the move from employee to business owner

Barb Stuhlemmer

Manor House

Library and Archives Canada
Cataloguing in Publication

Stuhlemmer, Barb, author

Entrepreneur awakening : making the move from employee to business owner / Barb Stuhlemmer.

ISBN 978-1-988058-28-3 (softcover).

ISBN 978-1-988058-29-0 (hardcover)

    1. Entrepreneurship. 2. Job satisfaction. 3. Success in business. 4. Quality of work life. 5. Work-life balance. I. Title.

HB615.S784 2017   658.4'21   C2017-906345-6

Printed and bound in Canada / First Edition.
Front Cover Illustration-design: Sarah Davis
Interior-layout: Michael Davie
Interior edit: Susan Crossman, Crossman Communications
192 pages. All rights reserved.
Published October 2017
Manor House Publishing Inc.
452 Cottingham Crescent, Ancaster, ON, L9G 3V6
www.manor-house.biz
(905) 648-2193

"This project has been made possible [in part] by the Government of Canada. *«Ce projet a été rendu possible [en partie] grâce au gouvernement du Canada.»*

Funded by the Government of Canada
Financé par le gouvernement du Canada

Contents

I dedicate this book to my husband Brian and my three children: Connor, Jack, and Chloe. It is because of you that I became a business owner so that I could work closer to home and be around when you needed me. It was with your blessing and support that I felt empowered to explore all that I was capable of creating in my business. It is with your ongoing love and understanding that I have been able to help hundreds of business owners step into their entrepreneurship and create a life they are passionate about.

Acknowledgements

There are a few people in my life who I have mentioned in this book as mentors or business friends, and several others who are not mentioned specifically but who have made a difference in both my business and my personal growth. I would like to acknowledge my gratitude to them for sharing their insights, their friendship, and their love with me through the development of my businesses over the years.

Thank you for being my friend, mentor, mastermind companion, and/or coach: Dana Pharant, Cindy Ashton, Rose Adams, Laura & Scott Gisborne, Jackie Ramler, Sarah Davis, Rich Grof, Theresa Dowsett, Fabienne Fredrickson, Deborah Foster-Stahle, Sue Cook, Amanda Sutton, Harold Wodlinger, Sydni Craig-Hart, Simone Usselman-Tod, and Jessy Morrison.

And to a very special friend, Susan Crossman, for your weekly support on our accountability calls over the years and your support of the development and editing of this book – I am so very grateful for your ongoing friendship. And to my publisher, Michael Davie and Manor House, for the crash course on book publishing and the patience required to help me learn what needed to get done.

Foreword

No matter what I did for others, no matter how well I understood their needs, no matter how much I listened or gave, no one in my life ever seemed to truly know or understand me.

I have felt that I was special from as early as I can remember and at about age five I decided that I would one day express myself as a scientist — one with a white lab coat.

I knew I was meant to help people, to understand their problems and offer solutions; I knew I was meant to lift people up and give them confidence when they felt they were not worthy.

For years, I was the person to whom my friends turned when they were going to hurt themselves, or wanted to run away, or when they felt insecure or misunderstood.

I felt I had a calling but, in time, I forgot. I forgot I was special. I forgot I was needed. I moved on to my love of science, and my white lab coat, and tried to find my path.

In high school I was not popular, but I hung-out with the popular crowd. I was not athletic, but I played on several teams.

I was not pretty, but I was always invited. I didn't fit in, but I was always welcome.

Most people can relate to a teen with self-confidence issues. I was smart, I was liked by most people and loved by many, and yet I never did anything to excel beyond my safe-zone, the place where I was comfortable, where I fit in, and where I could be seen as intelligent.

I was always looking for praise and yet I never gave it to myself. I wanted to climb the ladder of success and yet I never seemed to be able to encourage myself to try and achieve.

I followed the easiest path to accomplish the most I could, and it brought me some success, but not, ultimately, what I was really after. Something was missing and I didn't know what.

While my peers were just looking for part-time jobs, I was looking to answer a calling.

I didn't fit in with the "A-crowd" because they wanted to be doctors and lawyers and that seemed to me to be a lot of hard work with a defined cap on my growth.

Time passed and I entered the work force, I worked hard and made decent money. I became swept up in the busyness of job-marriage-and-mortgage that so many of us understand so well.

It wasn't until I was in my late 30s when I started to focus more on my kids that I began to recognize that I was not doing what I was supposed to be doing. You know what I'm talking about: I wasn't engaged in *my calling*. Did I even have one of those anymore?

I remembered that at one point I had thought I was special and I remembered that I had once expected to follow a calling... but I had never pursued the idea.

Could I be successful without a calling? Yes, but there was still something missing.

There were a lot of reasons why I had not generated more success. I didn't have a university degree. I didn't come from money. I didn't think I knew enough about anything to be able to add value. I didn't know what my passion was. I didn't think I had marketable skills.

The only thing I knew I had, was a drive to be around for my kids, to set an example for them that would inspire and encourage them. That drive helped me lose 76 pounds and start my own business.

It was a demanding time and I was full of questions. How could I make this work? Where was it leading? How would I make ends meet? How long would this idea of running a business last before I'd be back in a job?

On my journey from employee to entrepreneur and master business strategist I learned a few things about business and a lot about myself. So much so that I awakened to a new world of opportunities.

I realize now that I am not the same person I was 13 years ago.

I am now able to help more people, spend more time with my kids, have an incredible friendship with my husband, travel the world, learn all the time, live my life in "growth mode," with passion, and love more intensely.

Everything in my life has more colour and texture, more feeling and emotion.

If you are looking at your life and your business, and all you see is the routine of existence, maybe your world looks like this:

- Get up
- Get ready for work
- Go into work
- Have breaks and lunch
- Finish and go home
- Eat dinner
- Watch TV

- Go to bed
- Start again
- Wish for Friday

If this is your daily routine, and you suspect that you are called to a bigger, more interesting life, then maybe it is time for you to find your entrepreneurial awakening, too.

Maybe it's time for you to find your calling and create a business that will lead you to the discoveries of yourself and your world that will lead you to a more vibrant, exciting future.

I invite you to read on and, like me, find your way to uncovering and responding to the calling that is destined to shape and give purpose to your life.

There *is* more available to you in this world — and it's bound to be amazing. Now let's see how this all works...

The Entrepreneurial Awakening:

Lessons Learned From Employee to Entrepreneur ©

Entrepreneur – from Dictionary.reference.com:

"A person who organizes and manages any enterprise, especially a business, usually with considerable initiative and risk."

Barb Stuhlemmer's definition:

"A passionate person able to motivate themselves and others to take risks and participate in the creation and maintenance of a business enterprise."

Introduction

> *In corporate business, there is an expectation of success. But entrepreneurs are set up for failure. We need community, structure, and a way to interact with others so we can learn.*
> -**Tanya Raheel, Client and Catalyst for Women's Empowerment**

Over the years I have met thousands of business owners, some who were new to business and some who have been in business for many years. Some began by working on their dream, some were motivated by the desire to build a business in their area of expertise, and some cut their teeth in a family business. I have come to see that there are two very distinct types of business owners: those who "work in their business" and those who "work the business." The latter type of business owner requires the ability to run a business and also a fair bit of insight into the world of business. Business owners that "work the business" are not just working, they are on a path of awakening. This path takes more than knowledge, time, and money. This path is found quickly by some, slowly by many, and not at all by others. This path of awakening is the road less chosen and, once you're on it, there is no going back. You cannot unlearn the emotional, spiritual, physical, and mental states you reach along this journey and it puts you in with a group of unique people. Your life will never be the same once you have journeyed inside the mindset of the entrepreneur.

We live in a very special time that is marked by a lot of awakenings. We are awakening to the realization that our food is closely tied to our society's health—way more than we ever could have understood when we started accelerating the creation of genetically modified organisms (GMO).

We are awakening to how our health is tied to everything we do physically, energetically, and spiritually. Things that were once considered faith-based or too "woo woo" for the boardroom now have foundations in science, like the energy work of the HeartMath Institute[1].

We are awakening to the need for changes in our social and economic structure. Those of us raised in Western countries tend to believe that every country aspires to be like ours, with our style of economy. In a country like Canada, where unique intra-cultural systems foster different types of economies, it's clear that people aspire to be more like themselves than like others. There is also a tendency to believe that countries without high levels of natural resources, jobs, or education want hand-outs. I cringed as a teen watching the "Save the Children" commercials on TV, not understanding how I could really make a difference. It seemed like an insurmountable task. But when I heard a talk by Jennifer Jackley[2], the co-founder of microfinancing organization Kiva.org[3], I realized that a self-sustainable vision of business and the economy was possible. She made it happen. "People don't want a hand out, they want a hand up," Jackley says.

The economic changes wrought by the 2008 global banking crisis helped many people start to awaken to their own callings and realize that we were not put on this Earth to go to school, get good grades, and land a great job for life. That was all a myth, and questioning it led to other questions as well. Like how can we continue with our way of life if we cannot get a good job? Which factors are fundamentally valuable to our success? What do we have without gainful employment or the opportunity for a promotion?

---

[1] HeartMath www.heartmath.org
[2] Jennifer Jackley – TED.com "Poverty, Money – and Love"
[3] Kiva Microfinancing Company (www.kiva.org)

The Entrepreneurial Awakening is the movement to a success mindset that is empowered by passion, motivated by desire, driven by purpose, and sustainable through life-long learning and the need to create a business that can provide for ourselves and others. It is truly a holistic view of business and life as a continuous dance of growth, vision, and righteous work. It differs from the world of a business owner who has created a job for themselves and who:

- charges 20% more than they made as an employee because that is all they believe their clients will pay

- works over 50 hours a week for a business income that often does not break even.[4]

- doesn't actually pay themselves from the earnings of the business

- wishes they could make what they love to do pay off and

- knows that if they don't make it work they will have to go get a job… and that thought makes them feel sick

The Entrepreneurial Awakening empowers a person to stretch beyond their comfort zone to successfully do something they have never done before. It takes the fear out of the thought of risk and replaces it with opportunities and options to make things happen.

It helps people create something that makes them happy and grateful every day for the opportunity to do something that often feels like play. It's still work, but it is the work of Dharma, the work that pays back to those who are committed to it.

The good news is that there is a path and there are things a business owner can do to help navigate this transition.

---

[4] Small Business An Entrepreneur's Plan, 7th Enhanced Canadian Edition [2017]

Do you have to be an awakened entrepreneur to make money in business? No, but it is more fun, your life will feel more balanced, and the work is easier when you do reach this state.

Do you have to be "awakened" in order to be a good business owner and boss? No, but it will make the process of business growth, hiring, training, and employee buy-in more painless.

Do you have to be "awakened" to create and grow a small business into a multi-million-dollar, global corporation? Yes, I think you do. There is a time in the life of a business where simply knowing how to do the work is not enough.

In this book, I want to tell you about what I discovered on the journey to my entrepreneurial awakening, and hopefully show you how to be the person who does not just "simply do the work," but who truly envisions, invests, enables, and acquires all that is needed to create a business with a legacy. I have divided this book into three sections to help you see the course of this transformation:

Part I   Learn It

Part II   Implement It

Part III Live It

How It Works

As children, we spend most of our time in the "living" aspect of life. Of course, children have a great deal of life to learn, but they do not have to focus on, "now it's time to learn" or "I learned how to use a fork and I should practice it so I get better at it." They just live it. They accept every new idea and make up their own. They freely implement new skills and fail over and over...without feeling like a failure. Failure for a child is all part of being and growing.

Failure for a business owner, on the other hand, can be humiliating, discouraging, or an indicator of our inability to deliver excellence. Failure is about the lack of perfection and, even if one is not a perfectionist, having a business that is seen as credible and valuable requires a lot of excellence without failure.

What I want to share with you in this book about the journey from employee to entrepreneur is how failure is actually the building block of the most successful entrepreneurs in the world. I want to show you how others see this journey and I want to share what I personally have learned along this path.

I also want to give you insight into the three key areas of this transition that I mentioned earlier. Specifically, I would like to share with you:

1. What you need to fully learn so you can fit in to the entrepreneurial world and stand out as a business owner.

2. How to implement the basics so you will feel in control of your business and your life.

3. How to include "living" in everything you do so that your business and personal lives are so compatible that you truly enjoy the life you get to live.

Starting your own business is an incredibly courageous step. The tagline of Jena Rodriguez, of BrandwithJena.com, states this perfectly: "Entrepreneurship is NOT the easy way, it is the BRAVE way!" It's about the courage to start, to continue, and to grow. Transitioning into an entrepreneurial mindset is an awakening that takes a journey of self-identification, relationship, humility, and a touch of narcissism that allows you to focus on your beliefs about yourself. If you want to feel like you are not only the expert at what you do, but also that you are the expert at the development of your business, then read on. As Jena asks, "How big is your BRAVE?"

Not Awake?

What is it like to not be awake? Of course, it is not something you can see until you are out of it. Like being in a dream, you cannot tell you are in a dream until you wake up. I now recognize that I'm a very different person today than I was even 13 years ago. If you stood me beside my former self, you'd say we are sisters, but not at all the same person. My awakening was so extensive that it extended to my physical being as well.

I look back on my 20s and see something resembling arrogance in my approach to the world. Do you remember that, too? The 20-year-olds of my generation were reasonably well-educated adults, and we had all the answers; we set out to work this world. I remember feeling the freedom of adulthood. I could travel where I wanted. I could make big decisions. My path in the world was mine to choose. Should I go to school in my home town or away somewhere? Should I stay in this job or try something else? It was an exciting time for me as I took flight. But had I learned enough? Were we actually capable of doing whatever we wanted? Were there really opportunities for me to just pick up and start over again?

I know I was very focused on starting my career and my family after graduation. I did some traveling, but, getting started was my goal. I wanted stability, you know the kind,—like our parents had. I wanted the day-to-day responsibilities, the regular paycheque, the opportunity for promotion, and the prestige that came with a good job title. I wanted my family to say, "Oh Barb is working in the sciences," and know that their pride would be justified. I had been well-primed for a life with a job. I knew what it looked like and felt like because I had grown up in a family with two parents who had both been in the same jobs my entire childhood. Thinking I would land a great job after school was familiar and comfortable, but it turned out to not be very rewarding. Why did I know this? Because once I had my job after school I found that every three years or less, I would find myself in a new job.

There were many reasons for this, most of which I had no control over, or so I thought. Deep down I was eager to awake to something better, something longer-lasting and more fulfilling, but I didn't know what that was; I was just expecting change.

Awakening is an opening up to an understanding that was once unknown. It really refers to change.

Accepting the change from employee to business owner is your first step in an entrepreneurial awakening. As I became more awake, the rate of change in my understanding increased. There is no cap on knowledge. Although I have come a long way from those first days of business ownership I can see there is much I have yet to experience, and I accept that there are things I do not know that I do not know.

Another key to understanding is that an entrepreneurial awakening does not simply refer to business, it refers to all aspects of your life. A business prospect once asked me, "What if my problem with my business is not business related?"

"It often isn't," I answered. Our business and personal lives are two pieces of ourselves. If you try to keep them completely separate, you will struggle with life satisfaction. Integration and balance (if you can call it that) are important goals for your success in business and in life.

Giving and Receiving

As an employee, my focus was on the hours I had to put into my job and the pay that would come out of it. I showed up when I was expected and expected payment when I was promised.

I didn't have to negotiate my time or pay (until I wanted a vacation or a raise). I didn't have to constantly look for new employment. I was rarely alone and, importantly, I got benefits and could give to charity through my paycheque.

I was only connected to my community where my personal life took me – through my church, for example, or at the school my kids attended, through sporting events, or at the grocery store.

Doing something global meant giving to a global cause, like Greenpeace or Save the Children. My focus was inward, on myself, and I based what I deserved on what I gave. It was a reciprocal relationship based on expectation and equity.

I was a "pleaser;" someone who looks for self-satisfaction by pleasing others. Even friendships were self-centred and had a return on investment (ROI). If I gave enough, I would deserve the friendship. Not everyone experiences this level of dependency, but the focus here is on the fact that the employee mindset revolves around a dependency on getting because you give.

By contrast, my entrepreneurial focus is on growth, time management, client satisfaction, and making a difference. I work to create solutions and show up when I'm needed. I negotiate my prices and time, and I am constantly looking for new clients. I envision new markets and products and give back to my community through volunteer work, both personally and professionally, where I also gain credibility and strengthen my reputation for trustworthiness.

Running my business has a local impact and a cumulative global effect when combined with other businesses. I get to help others by providing something they need and, in return, I am helped through payment and the satisfaction of contribution.

This is true for all entrepreneurs, whether you are selling an O-ring that stops the tap from dripping, or providing services that enhance people's lifestyles. Entrepreneurialism is the greatest reciprocated gift you can create, especially when it is about consistently giving and receiving.

Part I - Learn It

I dream the dreams others said would not be possible.

- Howard Schultz, Chairman and CEO of Starbucks

Learning that entrepreneurship is a different way of thinking takes time. There are obviously some people who take to it faster than others, but it is available for all to learn. I believe that we have all met someone along the way, a friend, co-worker, or another person in school, who had a different drive, were less of a mainstream thinker, and who would come up with some idea to create a little more cash in their lives. When I attended school more than 25 years ago, the focus of education was strictly aligned with the industrial model (get a good education — get a good job)... but there were people with a different focus even then.

Now we have the internet and I love what I'm seeing. The internet has given us the ability to share our stories. Creative youth are sharing lots of stories. I have seen some very enterprising teenage entrepreneurs who have created viable businesses with ideas that they have brought to market. The internet has also allowed our youth (and everyone else) to reach a market they could not have hoped to reach previously. I was at an awards ceremony where I was blown away by what a young entrepreneur had been able to do with duct tape and an internet connection. She was ready to learn leverage—the step after The Basics—and she was not afraid to take the risk to make it all happen.

The subject of entrepreneurship has a broader scope than does the subject of business. Entrepreneurship requires internal observation and personal growth, as well as business development. As we go through the "Learn It" section of this book, we'll look back at employment, discover the importance of the Ego, and the challenge of loneliness, and I will share with you my top 10 required basics for starting a business: after all, entrepreneurs do have to know how to build a business!

Chapter 1: It's All About You (Ego)

You can veto any idea and create your own path.

- Barb Stuhlemmer

It's done — You've done it. You started a business to offer the world your expertise, your ideas, your amazing new discovery, your patented doo-dad, or whatever it is that your business service or product delivers. You took the risk and you launched the business. Like many new parents, there will be plenty of people with advice, suggestions, and insight, but you have the last say. You can veto any idea and create your own path.

When we start a business, we don't really think of ourselves as "being at the top." Yes, we have the final say, but what should we be investing in, focusing on, or actually *doing* with our time? There are so many things to learn as a new business owner, and so many ways to fail. Having that veto is a liability more than an earned responsibility. Of all the advice and information coming at you, what is best for your new business, and what should you ignore?

A total of 98.2% of employer businesses in Canada are small businesses[5] and they tend to opt for an attitude of "It's all about me." After all, it was your idea, and your money, your expertise, your time, and your sleepless nights that went into getting the business rolling. It IS all about you. Who else is going to care about your business's success as much as you do? Who else will put in the overtime and give up their weekends? Who else will give up taking a vacation for years? It's all about you because you are the one to make it happen, and you are the one who will sometimes feel alone in it.

---

[5] Innovation, Science and Economic Development Canada [August 2013) **Key Small Business Statistics**

To be able to manage your business, and continue to love it, you need to find the right people to share your dream with, and that will not be easy.

Tip #1: Friending your Employees

We spend a lot of time with our employees and sometimes our clients. It is often possible that we will befriend them as well. Is this right? Is this wrong? You might think, "I can't help it, I like people." This is great, but remember that when you need help and you turn to your employees or clients, you may not get the result or response you want. Why is this?

In relationships, we have boundaries. Some boundaries are set by social expectation and some are defined by agreement. The social expectation of an employee/boss relationship is that the boss manages the challenges, oversees the projects and plans, defines the expected direction, and ensures the bills get paid. The business owner/boss is the one taking the risks and responsibility for all of the financial debt and legal agreements. The employee delivers on the expectation to produce defined results in a set period of time in return for pay. If there is a big profit in the business, the owner is the one that will reap the reward, but if there is a big loss, then they are the ones dealing with the fallout. Either way, short of bankruptcy, the employee can expect to get paid.

When there is a problem in the business the employee may worry about the stability of their employment. They may even start looking for a new position with another company. In the chapter on Chapter 3: Employee Mindset (Deserving) I will go into more detail about the differences between what an employee expects in their relationship to your business. Even if they have loyalty to you, and feel they can help save your business, they will not go without a paycheque for long, if at all. So, it is just you at the top.

Friends without Benefits

Go ahead and befriend your employees. I believe we create a much better work environment if we like each other, but remember that there will be a limit to what you can share with them. If the day comes when you have to fire your friend, will you be able to do it? You cannot share your full business, personal struggle, and insider information with an employee, unless they are the vice president and are already shouldering the responsibility of the business's success and failure.

By having a boundary around your relationship, you will give them the ability to do what they do best in their position at the company, without worrying about the company. After all, you hired them in the first place for their specific expertise.

One of my clients runs a virtual support business. She has contractors to do various work for her clients and, being a friendly and kind person, she befriended her contractors. She'd have meetings to give them insight into the business. She'd give them autonomy to create new systems within her business. She'd connect them to her clients. AND she found that her business was exhausting her.

Ultimately, she realized that her contractors did not all think of her as a friend. They would grow their own businesses using the insights my client shared with them and then they would leave her when they were too busy to serve her interests. One even left and then connected with her clients later. They left because they did not want the responsibility of developing her business. They just wanted to be paid for their own expertise.

Trying to be friends and the boss is not easy, and it's not a good business model. Having great leaders in your business is better than having a business full of friends. Be a friendly leader, not a leader of friends.

Tip #2: Hire Intrapreneurs

What's an intrapreneur? These are people with excellent entrepreneurial skills that will use their insight, drive, and risk tolerance to help grow your business. Having people like this on your team will make running your business easier. If they are good, then your job will be less stressful as well.

Intrapreneurship can be described as a cross between initiative and ownership. We all look for that person who has the initiative to go beyond their prescribed duties to complete their tasks to a level beyond expectations.

But how do you get someone like this in your business? Answer: By hiring someone willing to take higher risks for him- or herself.

When I hired contractors for technical writing I was looking for engineers who liked to write. After I had identified their skill and done a "test month" of working with them, I would reveal my plan or what I saw as the future of my company, and it always included possible ownership.

My best contractor was someone I could completely trust with my clients and my projects. She would go above and beyond my expectations and I would pay her more than she felt she was worth. She knew that, as the business grew she could have part ownership if she wanted it and we could talk about what she saw that looking like when we got there.

When I was ready to step away from the company, I offered her part of the business. Although she was excited and driven to be intrapreneurial within the business, she was not interested in being entrepreneurial at all. It was the perfect relationship.

Tip #3: Clients Versus Friendship

Having clients as friends can be very difficult for you in your business. Decisions you make can affect their relationship with your business and then affect your friendship.

Again, the social expectation of friendship is very different from the business/customer relationship. Charging your friends, or not charging them, may end up feeling awkward and unfair to one or both of you.

When issues arise in the business, it may be even more difficult to remain friends, as service, product and price may need to change and your client/friend will be biased with regards to an outcome that would affect their purchase. For example, what if you had promised your friend/client that you would give them your time for free. What if they expected this time as a foundation for something else they must do to create income in their business? Now, what if you become so busy in your business that your time becomes more valuable? You do not have an hour to give away anymore. If you did have time, you would have to charge 10 times what it was originally worth.

Is the person a friend for whom you would continue to make time, or a client from whom you would expect payment? Do you feel good about the situation, or do you feel used?

Does your friend feel betrayed or your client grateful for all of the free time already given? It is complicated.

Selling to a friend is fine; confiding in them is more challenging. Unless they are also an experienced business owner, your friend/client may not have the knowledge, experience or insight to help you.

Your friend will want to see you do well because they like you, so they will try to give support in some way, even if they truly don't have the right answer. Our families do this for us as well.

If it comes in the form of advice, I recommend you evaluate their advice carefully (as you would with any advice) before you implement anything.

Advice given emotionally and without experiential context — and implemented blindly, without metrics and research — can ruin a business.

Tip #4: Family, Friends, and Peers as Confidants

As I mentioned, the above holds true for family and friends as well. Knowing you are struggling, or having "hard times," is difficult for the people who care for us and love us. It might even trigger the "get a job" response in spouses who fear losing what you have built together.

Confiding in your family and friends can make you feel guilty, fraudulent, unworthy, and incompetent. Was I wrong to expect my friends to understand?

$70k Is Underpaid – Really?

Some years ago I was at a place in my business where I felt I wanted to give up.

I was so stressed about my business's bills and debt that I decided to apply for a job. I had not worked full time for another company for about five years.

I updated my résumé and started searching for employment opportunities. I hated doing this, even when I had been an employee, but giving up on my dream and my independence made me feel like I was betraying myself.

I sent out a few résumés and immediately got a call from a recruiter who had a job prospect for me. After a short chat, he told me the pay and time commitment expectations.

Although this was a full-time employment position, the company expected the person in this position to be in the office every day. I would have to commute 1.5-hours each way in order to meet this expectation, which was not acceptable to me for five days a week.

They also wanted to hire me into this position as a contractor with no benefits, and there was an expectation that I would run all of my expenses through my own company.

For this opportunity, they were offering $35 per hour.

I was currently charging and billing $70 or more per hour in my company and I told him I was not willing to work for $35 an hour. The recruiter asked me what the lowest wage I was willing to accept was and I told him $55 an hour.

He sighed and told me that he knew his client would not go for that. Then he confided in me that he had received more than 200 résumés for the position under discussion and only two of the people, one being myself, had been qualified; neither of us was willing to work for the amount of money on offer. This statement made me feel great, because I was one of only two qualified applicants, but I was disappointed that I was expected to work for less than I could afford, and without any autonomy.

One afternoon shortly after this call, I was having lunch with two friends. One was a business owner who worked on commission and the other was a teacher who worked on contract. I was so frustrated about this situation that I told them the story.

After letting them know the details and how I felt, they looked at me in confusion and asked how much $35 an hour worked out to be for a year. I was stunned by the question but I replied with my estimate of just under $70,000.

They were not supportive and scolded me for implying that this was not enough money to live on, especially since I was having money trouble at the time.

Their estimate was correct that I could live on that amount of money, but since the billing would be run through my business, I'd still be required to do all the admin work of my business (e.g. collect taxes, get my bookkeeping done, pay for office materials, etc.), and I would not get paid for the 15 additional hours of commuting I was expected to make every week.

If you truly believe you have a great business idea, and you are on the right track, confiding in friends and family members who don't understand business risk and responsibilities will result in making you feel very alone and cut-off from the world.

Even chatting with other business owners, as described in my tale on the previous page, can make us feel this way.

When you reach a certain ability to understand and manage your business, you will run into new issues. Issues that someone who has never owned a business, or who is new to owning a business, will be unable to consider empathetically.

Asking advice of a new business owner who is less experienced than you can turn you into the supporter in the relationship. You will not be able to get the insights you need from them, and you will leave the conversation feeling unheard and unappreciated, or worse, feeling like you have been wasting your time; you might even feel like giving up.

Peers and Experts to the Rescue

Have you ever been to a meeting at your workplace as an employee and heard the room erupt into applause and cheers when someone said, "I quit my job today?" Likely not, and that is because employees usually only quit their jobs as the result of an adverse event.

Now, imagine that a room full of business owners are listening to a similar announcement. I cannot tell you how many times I have been present at a situation like this, and have heard cheers and applause as a new business owner finds the courage to step full-time into their business commitment. Business owners support each other!

Support for what you're doing needs to come from someone who is either going through the same experiences as you are, or who has done it before.

Find a mentor, join a mastermind group, create an advisory board and/or hire a coach. Just don't do this alone. You can *start* a business on your own but no one can *succeed* in business alone.

Tip #5: Peer-to-Peer Networks

Surround yourself with like-minded people who will support you when you are struggling, lift you up when you are down, and celebrate with you when you make great choices or accomplish something new.

The best way to do this is to attend local networking groups. Find one that you like and attend regularly so you can create connections and strong relationships with the people in the room.

This fostering of relationships will allow you to support them more deeply and it will create a relationship that will invite them to support you, too.

You don't have to take advice or insight from all of the people in the room.

Find one or two people you can easily spend time with, whose business idea and method of doing business you like, and who seem to have similar ideas, struggles, and experiences.

Now you will have someone with whom you can work through challenges. Someone who won't start with "get a job" when you are deflated, but who will help you look for solutions.

Tip #6: Working with an Expert

You should be paid for your expertise and you should pay for an expert's experience as well. When we start a business we often have more time than money.

If you have not budgeted for personal development, which, by the way, is your most effective investment into your company's biggest asset (you), then finding ways to learn and grow without money is key.

That said, here are three ways you can work with an expert for little or no financial cost to you.

1. Find a coach or expert who is teaching what you want to learn online and sign up for their newsletter, read their books, and follow their progress. The best of these coaches will often offer free seminars and programs online. Model what you see them doing and sign up for everything they give for free. If you can afford it, go to one of their low-cost events in person to be with the people who also need what is offered. You will be surrounded by your peers at this type of event.

2. Start your own advisory board. It is possible to get experts to agree to support your business growth.

My Advisory Board
About a year into my first business, a business expert I knew suggested I consider having my own advisory board. He gave me some information on what it might look like and I researched what was expected of both the advisors and the company they were supporting.
I found a contract and a model I could use and then I approached three people I respected in business, each of whom had different skills and areas of expertise. They also had a shared experience in SME manufacturing, my target industry. I asked them to volunteer their time and support me and my business for two years.
I initially felt like I was crazy to ask the VP of a car company, the former CFO of a pharmaceutical company,

---

> *and the coordinator for a government-supported entrepreneurial program, all with numerous other credentials and experiences, to commit two years to supporting me and my company. "Why would anyone do this?"*
>
> *I was thinking to myself. But they did, and they did it for two reasons:*
>
> *1. They knew and liked me and they were confident that I would create something valuable. I did have to show them my business model and current business operations before they would commit.*
>
> *2. They, like most successful people, love to give back and this was a perfect fit for what they liked to do.*
>
> *They signed a contract to meet three times a year for dinner (which I paid for) and discuss what I had done, what I was planning on doing, and what needed to change.*
>
> *It was a phenomenal experience, one of the greatest investments in my learning that I had achieved up to that point.*

3. Engage a mentor or be a mentor. Having a mentor is a great way to ensure that you are staying on track. They will see your potential and will often support you, even without you asking. I have been fortunate to have had many mentors over the course of my life. Recently, in the year I turned 50, I had the opportunity to visit a woman who had been a mentor to me in my teens. I still felt very strongly about her ability, and her place in my success, and I could see in her eyes the pride she felt knowing that she had been a part of what I had been able to achieve.

I told her how much I appreciated her support so that she knew how important the small things she had done for me had been, and how much she'd affected my life.

My Advisory Board – The Final Word
It was not until after I was finished working with my advisors on my self-developed advisory board that I started to truly understand why they had done what they did. There was a third and even bigger reason to be a mentor—one that I had not seen when they had signed up. This was the real reason that they were motivated to travel three times a year for a dinner, why they had felt one person and one company was worth their investment. As I started mentoring new business owners myself on a "pay-it-forward" basis, I started to see the answer. As a mentor, I was getting as much back as I was giving. Being a mentor for others was as important as having a mentor.

Hopefully, you can now see that you must focus on YOU as your business's biggest and best asset if you want to achieve growth and success.

Running your business is all about you but it doesn't need to include only you.

"We are not in business for ourselves. We are in business for our clients. Understanding this distinction will help keep a business owner focused on what they need to sell while understanding what their clients truly need or want. So, what do our clients want? They want an experience they can enjoy because if they get that, they will come back again and again. "

- Barb Stuhlemmer

Chapter 2: It's Not About You (Control)

Ask, "what is the best thing I am called to do?" If there is a bunch [of things to do] I will not be my best.
- Joel Osteen, Senior Pastor of Lakewood Church

You may own the business, run it, dream and worry about it, take the risks, and invest the money and time in it, but when it comes to what your business does, it is not all about you. It is about your clients. Don't ever lose sight of the real focus of your business, which is to serve your clients and to be profitable. To be a profitable business you must be able to sell your services and products, and to do this you must have clients that are willing to buy from you. So why do people buy from one business over another?

It's My Favourite Colour

As I went through my preparation to become a new business owner I belonged to groups and trained with other new business owners. I noticed that there was a mindset common among them, which was the idea that "If I like it, so will my clients." There is nothing more arrogant, or farther from the truth, than assuming that your preference is the same as that of your best or ideal client. I saw gaudy letterhead and business cards made with clipart that were embellished with the owner's favourite colour – because they liked it. I also saw:

- *Lavender branding that targeted corporations*

- *Flowers on letterhead destined for professional desks*

- *Unreadable, curly-Q fonts that whispered, "I'm artsy and cute"*

This just proved how disconnected these people were from their ideal clients. In fact, most had not put much effort into identifying their ideal client. When someone asked, "who is your ideal client?" many would answer "anybody."

- *Anybody with a spine (chiropractor)*
- *Anybody selling a house (real estate agent)*
- *Anybody that eats (cupcake baker)*
- *The real answer is not ANYBODY—ever!*

We are not in business for ourselves. We are in business for our clients. Understanding this distinction will help keep a business owner focused on what they need to sell while understanding what their clients truly need or want. So, what do our clients want? They want an experience they can enjoy because if they get that, they will come back again and again.

When you know exactly who your best client is, then you can then ask them what they expect to see when they shop for the product or service you or your competition offers.

Here are four things I feel can make a difference to a client's experience:

1. Location:

Your client needs to be able to find you in a location that is appealing to them and convenient. If you are not conveniently located, then you will need something extra to draw them to you. They want to feel welcome, whether they are at your location in an office, an online store, or speaking with you on a telephone call. They want your business to look the way they expect it to look, whether it is a clean, upscale spa or a plain, open warehouse. They want the environment to smell appealing, whether you are selling cleaning solutions or freshly baked bread.

They want your business to sound inviting, whether it's because a calm brook is trickling in the background or the top hits are playing loudly and with excitement on your phone message. They want to associate enjoyable tastes with your business, if taste is expected. The energy of the location must match your ideal client's expectations, whether they come to you for a massage or a workout. Your location must appeal to all of their senses in a way that will make them truly enjoy the experience of patronizing your business. If that piece is missing, there will be nothing to bring them back.

If they find a place they love better, for whatever reason, they will pay more money and drive past your place to go somewhere else to shop.

Lessons from a Big Business's Mistakes

In the two years leading up to 2014, Target Corporation., the second largest discount store retailer in the United States, had attempted to open in Canada. They chose locations, pricing, branding, and a sales model that had proven to be viable in the USA. The problem was that this was a different country with a different economy. People had different spending habits, and consumerism was subtly different. Target's assumption that Canada was so similar to the USA that nothing else really mattered was fatally incorrect for their Canadian launch. They had not taken the time to find out who their target market was in this country, or to determine what they had to do differently in order to create an experience people here would love.

As a Canadian, it was obvious to me from the day they opened their doors that this company was destined to fail, and it did, finally selling off its last inventory and store fixtures early in 2015. In my city, we have a massive brand new, now-empty store that takes up half a shopping centre. It is a shame for the city, the customer, and especially for the company that invested so much in development.

---

2. Price:

If you are targeting the average family, you will need to know that the middle class is shrinking and most families have less disposable income today than they did 20 years ago. Your pricing may need to reflect a lower average income for families, or you may need to know how to target an upper-middle class family with a higher-priced product. In this example, understanding your clients' household income and their desire to have what you are selling will help you decide how your pricing is defined. Selling a higher-priced item may reduce your market size, but it may mean you can sell in a very specific location with a higher concentration of your target market. Don't try to compete on price because there will always be someone willing to sell for less than you, and competing this way will take more effort and cost you more in the long run.

When I started my business, I was fortunate to get a government grant and a year of training and mentoring. I learned a lot about the basics of how to own and run a business, including the basics of pricing. The basics are not always a good place to start with pricing and here is why:

The basics usually look at the fundamentals of, for example, your competitor's pricing, your previous hourly wage as an employee, your costs, and so on. These are all valid and do check them out to get an understanding of your price.

What I found for service based businesses, however, was that as a business owner you will often impose a ceiling on your revenue that is tied to past employment income. I was taught a calculation that multiplies your wage by a certain amount to come out with a reasonable wage to charge as a consultant. And, as a new consultant, you cannot charge what other experienced consultants are charging, so you tend to keep your prices low. For product-based pricing, the calculation usually includes the cost of goods plus profit. These are the basics.

The problem with these two types of pricing is that they do not take into account your target market or *your* value. You cannot easily sell the cheapest bauble in an upscale store because the value does not match the brand and the brand is based on the customer's buying habits. Pricing must reflect who you want buying your product, as much as how much it costs to produce.

For instance, let's look at a service that revolves around selling a training program to a new entrepreneur. I've known many people who sell to new entrepreneurs and I know that there is a wide range of pricing that they will accept, depending on *their* priorities, not their service supplier's.

I know businesses that sell programs for $60 and they say, "I cannot raise the price because new business owners are reluctant to spend money." That may be true for some, but not for all new business owners. I know this for certain as I've seen a business that sells $25,000 programs to brand new business owners and I've seen people purchase it.

The business owners that price themselves at a position they "think" someone will pay will be stuck delivering to this customer for a long time. They will make money, but not a lot of it, and their ability to support leverage in their business, so they can grow, will be difficult.

A second issue I've seen too often occurs when businesses sell their services cheaply at first to try to break into a market. The challenge with this is that their clients and prospects will come to value them at that lower price and will likely not be willing to pay more for the same product when it comes time to change the pricing.

Business owners who start this way often get stuck here for a long time, working for little or no money and trying to simply offset their lack of income with more clients. These business owners end up burning out.

Solution

To ensure you can eventually leverage your business you need to understand how many programs or items you can sell at $2 or $60 or $25,000, to be able to grow. By growth I mean, hire someone, pay for new systems and software, open a new location, expand a manufacturing line, etc. If there is no possibility at your current price that you can ever make enough money to grow, then you may have taken on a business model that is impossible to leverage and a target market that is not truly viable. Make sure you have positioned your product to sell to the right people so you can eventually make money at it and create more in your business in the future.

To ensure you don't burn out trying to deliver your service too cheaply, I recommend starting with a "launch" pricing model. If you want to break into a market with a penetration price that will attract new clients, then make sure they know it is for a limited time. Try some of these introductory pricing models:

- *New Location sale price*

- *The first 100 customers*

- *This month only*

- *Introductory pricing*

This makes it easy to put your pricing up to the actual value after you are more established.

Note – If you have already identified that you started your pricing too low, and you think your clients won't pay higher prices, then try this:

Announce to all of your current clients that your prices are going up as of _[DATE]_.

Tell them that because they are such valued clients you will be holding their pricing at the current level for the next _[TIME LIMIT]_.

Charge all new clients the higher price and charge all current clients their current price.

AND Raise your current clients' prices when you said you would.

Understanding your value proposition and your target market, and charging the right amount for your product or service from the start will ensure you get the right clients.

It also means that they will appreciate your products and service at the beginning of your relationship, and for many years to come, because you built loyalty into your pricing!

3. Quality

If owning a business is not "all about you," then having a great product is not about what *you* think, it is about what your clients think.

New business owners usually feel a huge pride and passion around what we plan on offering. We have a product we know people need, because we've needed it before.

We have something that we know is exceptional, because we are experts and we've been working in our industry for years. What we often don't know is what our clients really want.

Dictionary.com says that "Quality is an essential or distinctive characteristic, property, or attribute." We can make a product or service distinct, but if we do not know what is essential for our clients, then we are not providing a product of quality for them...and it is all about them. If clients don't buy, we don't have a business.

I know from working in a number of businesses, including the heavily regulated medical device manufacturing industry, that business development in this industry follows very distinct steps.

One step is the creation of a requirements document. These documents detail the requirements the final product must meet to be of value to the end user; that's what makes it saleable. There are the "must-have" essential requirements and the "like-to-haves."

Successful businesses do not guess what these requirements are likely to be, especially in medical device manufacturing where manufacturing follows several years of development without sales.

During those development years, the company must pay engineers, regulatory companies, marketing specialists, development consultants, technical writers, and others. This is usually funded through venture capital (VC) investment. VC's do not invest in companies that don't know their market.

They invest because they want to make money, and that requires selling a quality product.

If you want to know you have a quality product, make sure you:

- Understand who you are selling to. Ask people who are your ideal customers the question, "What do you really want to buy?"

- Write a requirements list of what you will create so that when you are building your product or service you can refer to it and ensure you are on track to meet your customer's expectations.

Understanding your customers' needs and wants before you try to sell to them will ensure you create a quality product they will want to buy.

4. Desire Fulfillment

Remember that your business was created to give you income for doing what you do best, but the income is coming from the people who want to purchase what you have to offer. You work for them, and that means it is about them, not about you.

How do we create customer desires while continuing to fulfil the desire we have to do what we love?

I've told you a little about my other technical writing business, ClearComm Information Design. In this business, my key roles were to write contracts, learn the specific science of the client's business, and write technical documentation while managing contractors engaged in doing the same tasks as I did.

My desire was to help identify how the documents could be streamlined to save the company money and time, and help the company with strategies to manage the systems in their business. I was not hired to do this, however.

What the company desired from me was a manual that would get them through the regulatory audits of the U.S. Food and Drug Administration (FDA). Ultimately the business was successful at fulfilling the client's desire, but not mine.

Streamlining documents to save the company time and money was a great bonus I could add to my service but it wasn't what they wanted to pay me to do. My business became unfulfilling.

As it grew, it was hard to find time to satisfy all of my other roles and responsibilities as the CEO of my company, especially when there was no hope that the business would ever lead to the fulfilment of my own desire.

If you want to truly love what you do, you need to love what your clients truly want you to provide for them. Then doing the work will be more like play, and you will produce the things that will sell best as well.

"Barb Stuhlemmer's Entrepreneur Awakening is the guide book every entrepreneur should have. Barb states that being an entrepreneurship is the brave choice, and with the steps, strategies and tools featured in this book, the road to happiness and success is achievable."
- **Charmaine Hammond**, professional speaker, co-founder of Raise a Dream, president of Hammond International, and author of five award-winning, bestselling books

Chapter 3: Employee Mindset (Deserving)

> *The least deserving person is usually the most entitled.*
> - **Alan Robert Neal**, Author, *Stuck Where You Are*

An hour for lunch, two fifteen-minute breaks and a full-day's pay on statutory holidays. I remember how my work life was a constant tally. How much do I owe, how much is owed to me?

There are some stark differences between the way you thought and behaved as an employee and how you need to think and behave as an entrepreneur. Even if you worked like an intrapreneur (an employee with an entrepreneurial drive), there are a few things that you will do or expect as an entrepreneur now that you would not have previously expected.

When I started my first business I invested in a networking group that was specifically focused on helping me connect to potential clients. After all, the best way to get a new client is via referral. My company was focused on selling services to high-tech businesses and, after a while, I and two other members of the group decided to start another chapter of the group for B2B (business to business) members only so we could all be focused on businesses (and not consumers) as referrals. It was a perfect fit and it worked well until I changed my business and my focus to target business owners, rather than corporations.

"This shouldn't be too difficult," I thought. "After all, I have known this group of people for close to five years. I will teach them how I support business owners with my services as a business strategist and then they will know how to refer me."

Or so I thought. After close to a year in my new business I had not yet received a single referral for what should have been an easy connection. When I had a candid conversation with a long-time friend who was in our group, he told me, "I would never refer a business coach!" I was shocked. Why did he wait a year to tell me this? Why did he not understand the value? What had I done wrong in preparing my referral team?

When I did some evaluation later, I was surprised to discover that my networking group of almost 20 people was comprised of fewer than 25% business owners. Everyone else was working inside a larger business as a C-level executive or on commission, including my friend. What they did not know about was what we have been addressing in this book: the loneliness, the sleepless nights, the fear of losing everything, the risk tolerance, the isolation, the responsibility, etc. They were not living the reality of the small business owner so they could not easily understand why anyone would need a coach or strategist to help them create or grow a business.

Even my friend, who worked on commission selling for one of Canada's largest media companies, did not understand that he was technically a business owner. He never presented as one. He only joined the networking group because his company paid for it. He never did anything unless it was authorized by someone else first. He took his allotted vacation times because that was what he was entitled to take. He was deserving, but not empowered. He did not have any skin in the game, no real buy-in or decision-making authority, except over choosing to stay with the company or leave it. If the business failed, he'd lose his job, but nothing else.

Note: For those of you who are commission-based salespeople – you *are* a business owner and if you want to truly step into the empowered life of an entrepreneur I highly recommend you read *High Trust Selling: Make More Money in Less Time with Less Stress* by Todd Duncan.

There is a distinct difference between the way you felt as an employee and the way you need to feel and behave as an entrepreneur. You are the one who is taking the risks. You have the tough decisions to make. You will lose more than your job if you can't make it work. You will act and live differently.

Below is an interesting comparison between some of the mindset characteristics of an employee and those of the entrepreneur.

Table 1 Mindset (Employee vs Entrepreneur)

Employee	*Entrepreneur*
• You are expected to be at work for set hours per week	• You set the hours you need to complete the work
• What does it pay?	
• What is expected of me?	• What can I make?
	• What do I expect?
• Weekends off	• Off when I'm not working
• Bonus for extra work	
• Make a wage/salary	• Extra work may pay off
• If I lose my job I have to find a new one	• Create an investment
	• If I lose my company others may lose their job
• Benefits	
• They own me	• Insurance
• Trade for effort	• I own it
• Climb the ladder	• Investment
• Leave when I want	• Unlimited growth

• Write a resume • It's my time off • Work until the project is finished • What can I buy?	potential • Lose investment • Create marketing • When do you need it? • Do the project while getting more projects • How much do I invest?

What's Important to Me

The first steps in any business growth program is to look at your values and mission. The more aligned your business is with your own values, the easier it is to do the work. The more you understand what your true mission is, the faster you can become successful. This is not passion, this is the essence of who you are and why you do what you do.

Your Values

As an extreme example, think about the fact that most of us could not become a contract killer because our values on life and ethics and morals will not allow it. Your business is more subtle.

If you are very environmentally supportive, then being a bottled water manufacturer will not fit with your idea of environmental stewardship.

If you are strongly family-oriented, and you have kids, then starting a business that requires you to be away from home 80% of the time will deliver a lifetime of regrets. Don't just align with what you love to do today, make sure you also align with what you will be able to do in the future.

If you don't know what your values are, use Google to search for a lists of values. You should be able to come up with several. On these lists there will be hundreds of words describing different human values, like honesty, responsibility, family orientation, drive to succeed, etc. Read through an entire list and highlight anything that strongly applies to you. Go back through your highlighted words and make a new list of your top 10. From those top 10, circle three that you embody most often. From those three, try choosing just one.

What is your number one top value? Mine is honesty. Choosing to do something where I am required to tell people things they may not like, and to always be honest about it, has been a great learning experience for me. I've learned to deliver powerful, honest responses that don't hurt people's feelings, but rather empower and motivate them to get out of their routine and do something different. I've also had to learn that sometimes I don't have to share at all.

Your Mission

A mission statement in business is usually a short phrase or single sentence. If your mission gets too long it will be hard for you to remember. Google's mission is "to organize the world's information and make it universally accessible and useful." That is a powerful mission statement, as the level of trust required to get people to engage in their products, and give personal and corporate information to the company, is astronomical. Not only does each individual have to trust them (search history), so do the companies that use their products (Gmail and Calendar), and the governments (like China, with their customized search engine).

Every person that works for Google knows and understands the company's mission and ensures it is part of everything they do. It allows them to align what they do with how the company wants to be perceived in the world.

In addition to their mission statement is their motto, "Don't be evil." This adds to the values Google brings to their products and offers their employees.

One of my friends chose to work at Microsoft over Google because of the difference in the two companies' values. Each was offering a great job and amazing signing bonuses, but my friend chose to work at the company that fit best with his values. Your potential hires and/or clients may do that as well.

Your values and mission are important ways to define the "personality" of your company.

Another high value of mine is around relationships. One company I worked for seemed like a great company. They were new and they had benefitted from a lot of investment. They had state-of-the-art technology and a beautiful work environment. They paid their people very well and had great benefits.

I knew many of the people that worked there, so it had to be a great place to work. Boy, was I wrong!

And their 'Values' list, which they had posted strategically around the building, should have been my first clue. They had lots of amazing values around quality, customer support, and service, etc., but nothing in their values list or in their mission statement said anything about their employees or the work environment.

It wasn't until I started hearing the grumblings from the people that worked there that I realized this company was a modern-day slave house. They would hire people on salary, tell them they were expected to work 50-60 hours a week, provide no overtime pay, and withhold vacation time until the product employees were working on was complete (about 1.5 years). Employees had a very hard time with this focus and because of it they kept losing great employees. That is expensive for a company.

Chapter 4: The Basics (First Baby Syndrome)

> *"You can start a business on your own but no one can succeed in business alone."*
> **- Barb Stuhlemmer**

There are a few concrete requirements to starting a business, such as a business name and a logo, an email address and a website, etc. And although we can start a business with very little investment or training, and very few assets, what does that cost us in terms of our business growth?

In the section of this book entitled, "It's Not All About You," I mentioned I had been awarded a government grant to start my business, and it came with a year of training and support. It was a valuable way to start to understand all of the pieces needed to start and run a business, and I'm going to explain many of them in this chapter.

One thing I am not going to talk about here, however, are the legal requirements of your business, since they vary significantly from one city, province, state and country to another. You will also need to look into your area's insurance, licensing and contract requirements, as well as HR policies, employment law, taxes, and a number of other issues that might vary from one jurisdiction to another.

I did learn all of the above in the training I undertook, as it was specific to my region. Each person in the program with me was building their business in and around the same city. I once taught business basics in Toronto for a group of people that came from about 10 different regions. The difference in resources available to them was huge, and it was impossible for me to reference all of them.

My recommendation is to find someone local, maybe within the economic development office of your city or town, and ask them what resources are available for new business startups; then reach out to the people supporting new business growth in your area, like your Chamber of Commerce or Board of Trade, government programming agency, or private venture centre. It is worth your time, even if you have to pay for it.

What Are the Real Basics of Starting a Business?

There will always be things you will need to learn, implement, and change as you build your business, but starting out involves some basics in the areas of business and personal growth.

For example, many business owners who are still in an employee mindset lack a clear brand. "Phew," some of you may be saying, "I have my logo, I'm OK there!" Not quite. By brand I mean any aspect of your business that can be experienced by anyone who interacts with your business, and that includes your customer. Brand is part of the basics and here is the complete list I will cover in this book.

1. A niched target market
2. A target-specific business name
3. A website
4. A domain you own
5. An email address connected to your domain
6. A logo/font/colour that represents your brand.
7. A business bank account
8. A business phone
9. A product or service to sell
10. A plan

I'll cover each of these in detail so it will be easier to understand the impact the items have on your business and how important it is for you to get these pieces in place when you start.

1. Niched Target Market

I know that you have likely heard this but I am going to say it again – **You cannot sell to everyone OR "anyone**." If this is your answer to the question of who could use your services, then you are in trouble.

Know exactly who your best client is, why they are drawn to you and your company, why they need or want your products, and where you will find them. The narrower you can make this definition at the beginning of your business, the easier it will be to sell to that market and the less you will have to spend on marketing. This does not stop you from actually selling to other people, it is just narrowing your marketing message to be succinct so it is heard clearly by your best potential customer.

- Selling to people who like to fish is very different from selling all-inclusive travel adventures to fly-fishers.

- Selling to women who wear makeup is very different from selling skin care to teens.

- Selling life coaching to people who are undergoing change is very different from selling to out-of-work baby boomers transitioning into a new career.

Although there are fewer people in each of the niches described above, they are going to be much more interested in what you have to say and sell when they know you are focused on their needs. People want to feel like they are understood. If you want to sell to everyone, then you will be up against some retail giants like Canadian Tire, Walgreens, and Walmart, and they compete on price with a huge buying power you likely cannot match.

When I ask small business owners who their target audience is, I often get the answer, "well, anyone can really use what I sell." I cringe every time I hear this because I know they have not thought this statement through. Even if you are selling water and you know everyone needs water, not everyone will be in your target market. People buy bottled water for different reasons, and knowing who buys bottled water, and why, will help you understand who your customer really is. This helps you create marketing language that will be specific to them.

Example: Bottled Water

Who could use it? *Everyone drinks water but not everyone will buy bottled water.*

Who Buys Bottled Water? *People with busy lives who are always running around, people who live in areas with high minerals in their drinking water, people who are afraid of their tap water, people in sports, people with kids, people who host events.*

Discussion:

If you pictured what each person above might look like, then you likely saw a different person for each description. To me, the person running around looks like a mom in a van. The people that live in an area with high minerals may have different lifestyles, but they live in the same region. Not all of them will buy bottled water, only those who are health conscious and aware that high levels of calcium or other minerals can affect their overall wellness.

The marketing for the first group (people running around) could target moms across several regions/provinces/states/countries. The second market would be localized to regions you would have identified as high-risk.

Now think about the language you would use to reach "moms on the go" versus wellness-focused individuals in regions where drinking water has a high mineral content. Would you be saying the same thing in the same way? No! And this is why it is so important that you never assume you are selling to everyone or anyone. Be specific.

---

2. Brand Specific Business Name and Language

There are a lot of different schools of thought on how to name your business. Do you give it your personal name (e.g. Jen's Promotions or Smith Accounting Services)? Do you use a unique industry name like, (e.g.) Anandam Wellness? Do you create your own words out of names or places (e.g. Brijen Shipping)?

Any of these can be the right choice if your target client will remember it. The key is to use words, phrases or compilations that will be recognizable and memorable, and that will represent what you are and do.

This is the same for the language and words you use for your brand. How do you describe your business, who you are, and what you offer? How do you want others to describe your business? Again, these words need to resonate with your target market. If you are using words that are unfamiliar to your market to describe what you do, it will be much harder to sell what you offer. You will clearly feel this if you find yourself constantly having to describe what you do. Unless you are starting an entirely new industry or science, you will likely never have to be in constant education mode.

When I started my second company I had already spent a great deal of time discovering what it meant to brand my first business. I had taken numerous courses and training programs, worked with marketing coaches, and read many books.

I also had to rename my first company because of a possible trademark infringement, so going through the naming and language discovery process had allowed me to develop a process that worked well. Let me share that process with you so you can discover your own language for your marketing and brand.

Grab a piece of paper or journal to capture your ideas. I recommend you invite some people to help you brainstorm your ideas with you.

1. Start by creating words that answer these key questions about your business and your clients: who, what, why, when, where, and how. Just write single words or short phrases that answer these questions.

For Example:

Who = women,

When = approaching, during, and after menopause

What = anti-hormone therapy

Why = reduce symptoms

How = in home

For this example, you may have many words for "Who," like mother, professional, executive, young mindset, etc.

Capture all the words that answer these five questions.

Note – remember that there may be an additional option to add a word that is specific to your industry, your family, or to you. Add that word to the list as well.

2. After you have these words, take out a thesaurus and start generating several lists of synonyms for each word. You may end up with several pages of words.

3. Now use your values or mission statement to go through this list and circle the words that are in alignment with it.

4. Use a brainstorming group (a group of invited people that will help you generate lots of ideas) to help you target the words that best fit your industry, your target market, and your business mission and values.

5. Start putting words together in phrases or compilations and create a list of possible business names.

6. Get your brainstorming group, your potential clients, or other outsiders to help you narrow down your choices and then choose a short list.

7. Go on the internet and check for similar businesses or product names and available website domains. Your business will be easier to find by people who remember the name if the website has a similar name. You also do not want to end up with any trademark issues.

8. Choose your name. It's important to have a unique name that you can use legally. I can share three stories of trademark issues that potentially cost companies thousands of dollars and required time to rebuild their brand image.

Story #1: Too close to my product

My first company was named SoftDoc Training Solutions. My company provided training and technical writing for the software industry.

SoftDoc was also the registered trademark name of a software program created by a Toronto company for the legal industry. I was not in competition with them and we were selling fundamentally different items.

I was able to register the name without issue because it was not another company's name. When I went to incorporate my company two years into my business, I decided to call the company that owned the software to let them know. They had been following me and although they felt, as I did, that we were not in competition, their clients were sometimes confused when they ended up on my website. Confusion is not a good thing when your name is confused with a registered trademarked name belonging to someone else. I did not want to be attracting their clients and they were not going to let me. Without argument, I changed my company name.

Story #2: I See You

My second story is about a company that ran its business under the owner's name. It had a training program that was very popular with new business owners. The owner had run this business for about seven or eight years and this program was only sold locally in one city. When the owner decided to start using social media, she was so well-loved and well-followed that anyone searching for her program name (not her company name) would find her. The problem was, her program name was a perfect match for a product of an incorporated company in Eastern Canada that had a registered trademark for that name. This company had been watching her for many years and had no issue with her. They are a global software development business that was also trying to increase their brand recognition online.

The training program that was delivered and sold locally had a bigger following online than the global software company. The problem was that potential clients of the software company were becoming increasingly confused when they did an online search, as they were finding the training company, rather than the software development company. The bigger issue was that the owner of the software company could not get any online traction for his own marketing because of the training company's successful use of the name.

The owner of the software development company contacted the owner of the training company to chat about the name and to ask nicely for them to stop using the trademarked name. It was not a horrible, angry discussion. In fact, the training company owner flew out east for a meeting and the two business owners eventually became friends. The training company ultimately did change its program's name. When the owner of the training company tried to sell the business, she realized she now had no brand recognition with the new name and that mistake cost more than expected.

Rebranding your best product is always a costly endeavor. Doing it while you are trying to sell your business reduces the value of the company and costs you even more because the new name has no brand recognition and thus no saleable value.

Story #3 Too Much PR

This story is quite new and I don't know the outcome yet, but it was a powerful reminder that even the best PR people can get it wrong.

A friend of mine who has been in TV production for many years recently created a women's association. She is very well-liked and respected by her community of big-thinkers and doers, so she attracts a lot of women who want to be in her circle of friends.

This lady launched a new association and its inaugural event was very well attended. Some very big names from the television world showed up, as well as a number of successful entrepreneurs and powerful people in different industries.

After the launch, there was a lot of online buzz about how great the event was, how high the energy had been, the amazing connections people had made, etc.

And then, one person posted a shocker. "Your association name is a registered trademark," they said. "You will likely get a call [from our legal department]." It took me 30 seconds to find the company and determine that the name was a registered trademark name. Oh yes, she was in the exact same industry, targeting the same people, and offering a similar experience. She is likely going to get a legal notice.

What a shame – she had spent several months making that event perfect, branding the new name, and setting up resources and connections. She invited the right people, attracted amazing speakers and went all out to do things right.
She had been very professional and spent months working on a project that will likely cost her months more work as she re-brands her association. And all of this could have been avoided with a 30-second check online for the name she wanted to use.

3. Domain Name

Yes, you need to own your own website domain name address. This is the part of your website address that follows "www" and it includes the ".com" or other extension. For instance, one of my domain names is blitzbusinesssuccess.com. I own this.

Below are two tips for generating your domain name: keep it simple and as short as possible.

Tip - As Short as Possible

There are plenty of tools—like bitly.com—for shortening a link that contains a long website address, and there are ways to remember websites so you don't have to type complicated addresses over and over: auto-fill in your web browser is a good example. But there are still some good reasons for trying to have a shorter website, especially if it is not exactly the same as your business name.

You want a short name so it will fit in other documents and applications. For instance, government documents may not provide enough space to write out a very long address. Also, if you want your full address to show, as opposed to a shortened link, in micro-posts, like Twitter, then it needs to be shorter. The longer your website name the harder it is to remember, and the more difficult it is to use it in media in its original form.

Tip - Keep it Simple

Many names are no longer available as a ".com" domain. This means we have to be a little creative in our naming. But be careful: if you use strange spelling for words in your domain address to make it short, people may make mistakes and be unable to get to your website.

For instance, don't use GR8 for the word "great" or any other texting short forms that change what we expect to see, unless you plan on pushing out a big marketing campaign to make the unusual spelling recognizable—like *www.zappos.com*, for example. (Note: This applies to your business name as well).

Typing help: Google might not recognize an unusual web address or business name the first time someone types it, so it must be spelled correctly, in full.

After someone has typed it once, today's browsers will remember past addresses and give them a list of possibilities from which to choose. This list will include the specific page(s) they have visited previously. Once the web address has been entered, your clients won't have to type it again unless they clear their browser cookies or move to a different computer.

Although long addresses are not good for social media, they truly don't matter for browsers and links. If you are stuck with a long name, you can purchase something unusual and shorter for social media that points to your website.

Setup help: A lot of interesting things are happening with social media, browsers, web sales, and advertising, and it is all changing quickly. I highly recommend getting an expert to help you define and set up your domain to match your brand and to help you develop a marketing focus for it.

4. A Website (and other online "real estate")

When I started in business I used to tell business owners that it was up to them to decide if they wanted to put their business online or not. In the early 2000's, website design was still very pricey and it was out of reach for many small businesses. That is not the case today.

Today, when asked, I now tell my clients, that they MUST have an online presence, and a basic website is necessary.

Clients and prospects must be able to find you online even if you don't plan on selling online.

If your business is completely invisible online, then it is literally impossible for your clients to get in touch with you.

With the extinction of the telephone book containing the Yellow Pages, consumers cannot find you if you don't show up online.

In 2010 some friends moved from my city to Ottawa, a five-hour drive away. They realized that there were a number of items they did not want to take with them and they began looking for a junk removal company to come and give them a quote for removing their unwanted belongings.

A business acquaintance, whom I really liked, owned a junk removal company and I thought this would be a good fit for my friends.

Unfortunately, I had lost my acquaintance's contact information. I looked him up online but I could not find his business. He did not own the domain name for his business name. His business name did not come up in a search with his personal name. I tried finding him through the database of the association to which we both belonged, but he was no longer a member. I knew where one of his signs had been posted around town, but when I got there I realized the sign was too small to read and I could not stop to read the sign and take down the number while driving. I was sure he had gone out of business.

Two weeks after I gave my friend the name of the national brand company to call, I saw the owner. He was still in business – "But not for long," I was thinking. How could he expect to stay in business and compete with a national brand if he could not be found online?

What can you do to start? Here are three of the easiest ways you can get started with online marketing:

a) Set up a simple website page using your domain name.

b) Create a business page on Facebook or LinkedIn.

c) Establish a personal profile on LinkedIn, Facebook and/or Twitter.

More complex online brand investments include:

a) Developing an interactive website with a blog or shopping cart

b) Writing articles for other online locations, like news feeds or affiliate websites

c) Joining groups online and participating in the conversations they host

d) Retweeting, sharing, and liking other people's posts

e) Setting up a YouTube channel and populating it with videos

f) Hosting a seminar or webinar online

g) Generating interview requests for online TV or radio shows

Don't let your business fail before your prospects have a chance to do business with you. Let them know where you are, how they can contact you, when you are available, what your main products are, and who you serve.

Check the Resources section at the end of this book for ideas on where to buy a domain name.

5. Email Address

A business email address is a must as well. This is not your cutesy Gmail account. You may be able to get your business name "@gmail.com" and that is a start, but if you own your domain name you will often be entitled to one email account for little or no cost, so there is really no excuse to avoid looking like a real business.

The fact that you have your own email with your domain name in it will show that you own the company and it will give you more credibility with prospective customers.

6. Brand Image

Your brand image needs to reflect the feeling you want people to experience every time they come in contact with anything representing your business. This includes your website, business cards, uniforms, store front, vehicles, signage, your spoken message, voicemail, phone scripts, sponsorships, social media, email signature, brochures, etc.

Representatives of graphic design companies that produce printed and image-related marketing materials will say that a business brand is represented by any image your clients and prospects experience. This is your "brand image," but I would argue that your brand is *every* sensory experience your clients and prospects have with you, including smell, taste, touch, sound, and, of, course your visual brand image.

Think about the experience you have walking into a grocery store that has an on-site bakery. My personal brand experience with them includes the incredible smells I get, warm and welcoming, when I enter the store. That is the experience I share with others when I tell someone about the store's great breads and it's part of what entices me to shop there again.

Creating a brand image takes a great deal of insight into your business focus and your target client. If you do not understand this process I would recommend hiring an expert to help you develop your brand and brand image.

When I started my first business I did it "on the cheap." I had defined my brand with little development or research and I asked a friend to create my logo at a cost of about $200. My image was OK but not strong or recognizable.

But when I rebranded and renamed my company due to the potential trademark infringement I mentioned earlier, I hired a graphic design company to do the work.

My brand development and logo design and marketing collateral cost me about $1600. This did not include any of the printing. My brand was strong, professional, and a perfect match for the relationship I wanted my clients to experience.

When it came time to do the branding for my current business, I had the expertise and training to do the brand development work myself.

I hired an expert to create the logo, which cost me about $700, and now I have a brand image that is instantly recognizable and has staying power with people who experience it. Often people will recognize my brand, which includes my image, before we meet.

Prior to creating my brand, I put a great deal of effort into identifying my target market.

After that, I needed to define exactly what I was offering, finalize my product and confirm my price positioning. When I thought about this I had questions like: Am I the cheapest, the most expensive, or the easiest? Do I offer the shortest programs or the ones that are the most involved? Do I do the work for people or get them to do it themselves?

Answer these questions to help you start the process:

- **Who are your clients?** Be very specific about this. Learn as much about them as possible. I know that my clients are small business owners who have a business they have been running for a while. They are knowledgeable about their products and services, in fact I would call them experts. They love being in business for themselves and have already attained some success, but they are challenged to make more money and grow their business. And most of all, they have an unstoppable desire to create a larger business in a bigger market, selling more, helping more clients, etc. I also know their personal demographics and the demographics of their businesses.

- **What do they need?** Not just what do you want to sell to your potential clients, but what are their needs and desires? My clients' biggest two needs centre around the fact that they need employees but they cannot afford to hire anyone and they want to help more people and sell more, but there are no more hours in their day to devote to new plans for growth.

- **What are you offering?** Your products and services must meet your ideal client's needs. I have seen many people who think they have an incredible, saleable idea for a product but when they create it, people don't buy. If you have ever watched the TV Show Dragon's Den or Shark Tank you will have seen this as well. In my first business, I offered a consulting retainer. Thankfully, I had a friend in a senior position in this industry and with his feedback I found out why I could not sell this product: it was not needed. Because of this information I made some tweaks and focused on what they did need and I continually landed $5,000 - $20,000 contracts. Your product offering must be specifically designed for the people you want to serve.

7. A Business Bank Account

Your business also MUST have a bank account that is separate from your personal bank account. Even if you are not a corporation, your personal money and your businesses money should never go into the same place. If you put personal money into your business banking, it is an investment. If you take it out, it is an owner's draw of some sort. You can use a personal account in your name if you are a sole-proprietorship, but it must be kept separate from your personal money. Corporations must have a business account.

The key here is "separate." Do not use a personal account for your money and your businesses as well. You do not want the CRA (Canadian Revenue Agency) or the IRS (Internal Revenue Service) charging you with tax fraud or sending you a bill for taxes you owe in your business which was really personal money for which you had already paid taxes. Make it clear, for them and for you, which money belongs where. Also, as your business grows, and more people come into your company, you will not want any confusion as to which money belongs to you, your business, or others.

One of the cheapest ways to help keep this clear, after you have your bank account set up, is to hire a bookkeeper. People are often surprised at how affordable this service is and it is usually one of the first things I get my clients to do when they are struggling to grow.

8. A Business Phone

For a small business, having a business line can be expensive. With business landlines or cell packages, getting the services you need is an investment in the smooth operation of your company. Do some research into prices and your needs, and then budget your expenses to include this absolutely essential service. Do not use your home phone!

My Mommy's Not Home

I once had a hair stylist who worked out of her home. She was amazing and talented, she was local, and she was reasonably priced. People would give me great compliments on my hair and I would give her the kudos, as I was thrilled to have this type of a consistent experience. I had one issue with her service, however, and that related to her phone. Whenever I called, and she was not home to answer the phone, someone in her family would pick up the line. No one responded with her business name, so the first time I called I wasn't even sure I'd called the right place.

When one of the stylist's kids answered the phone, they would simply say she was not home at the time and they would ask me to call back. Eventually a friend I had referred to my stylist had a bad experience that motivated me to stop using this lovely lady's services. My friend Sarah had called to make an appointment. The hairstylist's husband had answered the phone. It was quite obvious to Sarah that she had disturbed him. Here is the conversation as I remember it:
Husband: Hi

Sarah: Oh, Hi – I thought I was calling a hair salon?

Husband: She is working at the hospital right now.

Sarah: OK, ummmm…

Husband: You'll have to call back – CLICK!

And that was the last time I went to her or recommended her to anyone. If your clients are not going to get the treatment they deserve when they connect with you on a business basis, they won't do business with you. After all, what does this experience say for your brand? To me it said, "I'm not really invested in doing this, and neither is my family."

Be invested in your business, get a business phone.

Three Ideas for Getting a Phone

Other than simply paying for a business line, here are three ways you can get a phone so your clients will know that they are reaching an actual business.

a) Try this: If you have a landline in your home you can purchase a second number that will ring differently than the first one. Then tell everyone in the house that they are not allowed to answer that second ring. Set up your voicemail to say "You have reached Sandy's Salon and the Smith's. Press 1 for Sandy's Salon, otherwise stay on the line to leave a message for the Smith family." It is OK to appear as a small business operating out of your home, just make sure your clients and prospects can reach you when they need to.

b) Look into a Voice Over Internet Protocol (VoIP) telephone. Many cable companies, like Rogers in Canada, have a home phone line that is VoIP. You will get a completely separate line from your home line at a much reduced price and it will have all the features you need, like voicemail, call waiting, hold, etc. This will also give you great deals on long distance calling as well.

c) The third way you can ensure that you have a phone for your business is to get a business cell phone. Cell phone charges in Canada can be quite expensive, so make sure you have a plan that will cover your typical use. This might include unlimited daytime calls, unlimited texting, a suitable data package, etc. You may have to adjust this as you discover what your typical usage is.

Something else you will want is a great long-distance plan. I can't tell you how unimpressed I am when someone who is in business complains that they have to make a long-distance call.

My plan, which is included in both of my VoIP phone lines costs me $35/month and gives me unlimited free calling throughout North America, and many other countries as well. FREE!

If you don't have a great long-distance plan, then use an online alternative to a phone. These are all free or close to free:

a) Text messaging

b) Instant messaging (like Facebook or Google chat)

c) Skype

d) Purchase a phone card with cheap long distance

There is no excuse for not being able to afford to connect with someone in another city, province, state, or country.

9. Product or Service

This sounds too simple. "Of course I have a product," you might be thinking. "Why else would I start a business?" True, but if you are trying to sell something people don't want or need, then you don't really have something to sell. You need to do some research on your product offering, the price and place to sell it, your target market's needs, and your competition to know if you really have something worth selling.

I have found that in the coaching industry there is an overwhelming misunderstanding of what a client wants and needs to purchase. One of the biggest mistakes is to sell something that equates to a "dollars per hour" service. I know because I made this mistake. When I started my business, I had a one-month program, a three-month program, and a six-month program. The three-month program was three times more expensive than the one-month program and the six-month program was twice as expensive as the three-month program.

If you did the calculation you could determine exactly what I was charging per hour. People would ask if they could just purchase an hour for $100.

And how could I sell a six-month commitment when someone could simply purchase my services by the month, quitting whenever they felt like it?

The challenge with this was that there did not seem to be any value in what I offered. Quit-when-you-want coaching does not hold much credibility for accountability. It was not a product worth selling, because it was not a product worth buying.

Understanding what your value is will represent a good start in creating a product worth purchasing.

Knowing what your clients will experience, and ultimately take away, will help you position and price your products. Being totally clear on your costs and expenses will ensure you don't sell your product for less than the cost of producing it. Believe me when I tell you that this happens more often than you would think, especially when selling a service.

Just because you are willing to work for $20 an hour does not mean that $20 an hour is enough to cover your costs.

Don't forget that when you are in business for yourself you have to pay for your time and also the time you put into marketing, selling, administration, operations, networking, etc. And if you have inventory or other expenses, you must cover those costs as well.

I have several computers I had to purchase and there are maintenance costs associated with that computer. I also have an office in my home, a leased vehicle, networking expenses, online expenses (like hosting a website), etc.

I may not own a building, nor do I have a payroll, but there are still expenses that must get paid. At the very least, make sure you cover your costs and then add your payment price on top.

10. A Plan

This is a tough item for many people to complete because the idea of sitting in front of a computer to type out a 30- to 60-page business plan can be intimidating. You can take a plan to your bank as part of a request for funding. But you don't have to do that! The good news is that your plan is there to help you stay on track.

It contains your metrics and your goals, your mission and your ideas, your path and your perceived needs. It will help you avoid problems and it will help you stay focused on your vision so you don't get distracted by the shiny objects of new and interesting ideas that will start popping into your head regularly as you become more entrepreneurial.

I want you to know it does not have to be so detailed as to get you an investor or a loan. But it does need to be written. Here's a short overview of how to create something quickly that will help you manage your business and stay on track:

Start at The End

Define your business as you envision it 10 years from now. This will help you understand what you are truly missing in your business right now. List the tasks that you will need to complete in order to get to the 10-year mark and decide what you can do in the next year of business that will help you move towards your ultimate goal. Detail everything about your business that you will have had to create or accomplish to reach your one-year goal. You want to define:

- Gross sales per month
- Number of employees or contracts
- Estimated costs
- Number of products/services to offer

- Location/office size
- Marketing campaigns
- Clients (name them if you can)
- Average sales value

Be as specific as you can. The more specific you get the easier it is to create a plan to make it all happen.

Work Backwards

a) How much would you have to sell to reach your gross monthly sales? Do the math!

Let's use an example with real numbers. If your product sells for $250 and you estimate you want $2,500 in sales per month, then you need to sell 10 units.

b) How many people do you have to speak with to get one sale? Knowing your sales-to-prospect ratio will help you with this number.

If you have to make 10 calls to get one sale, then you need to make 100 calls per month to sell $2,500 worth of product.

Where will you get 100 names per month to call? What are the marketing actions you are going to take to fill your sales funnel?

To get a person to build enough trust to purchase from you they need to have between seven and 20 touches from your marketing efforts. That means each one of the 100 people you contact needs to see you or your brand at least seven times before you can even start asking for a sale. That is 700 touchpoints per month. (Touchpoints are "any aspect of your business that can be experienced by anyone that interacts with your business, including your customer.")

c) How will you reach your clients?

Determine your monthly marketing plan to deliver seven touches to each of the 100 prospects in your target audience over the month.

You will also need a client management program to collect the names of the prospects with whom you must follow up so you can manage your sales process.

Finally – write it down! Thinking about doing something is not enough to make it happen. If you write it down, you get it out of your head and give it a structure. If you really want to make it real, give a copy to someone else to review for you. Limit your plan to just a few pages of content so you can quickly look it over occasionally and identify if you are on track.

The Final Say on Basics

This was a very quick overview of the basics. I was fortunate when I started my first business to have received a government grant through the Self-Employment Benefits program: this not only gave me some financial support to start my business, but also training, coaching and mentor support. I highly recommend getting training at the start-up stage of your business to help solidify the basics and help you realize what is typical and expected, and what to avoid. Always have mentoring support. No great entrepreneur ever built their empire alone. In fact, most attribute their success to the people they have on their team, including their peers, mentors, and those working in their business. If you don't have someone to call when things are not going right, and I guarantee this time will come, then you will be less able to overcome the challenges and survive as a business.

Reading Recommendation:

For a step-by-step guide to the basics of business development and startups I Irefer you to the textbook *Small Business: An Entrepreneur's Plan* by Ron Knowles and Chris Castillo.

Chapter 5: Make Room for Errors

There are risks and costs to action. But they are far less than the long-range risks of comfortable inaction.
- John F. Kennedy

Making mistakes and being wrong are hard to accept. Most of us want to try to be right. We want people to see us as competent. The challenge with this mindset is that it sometimes limits our ability to change. Trying something new means we have to do something we have not done before, and that means we are not competent at it yet. This is when our desire for comfort can override our need to change, and we stay stuck.

I remember meeting Rose Adams, now a good friend of mine, in the first year of my business. Rose had (and still has) the presence of a leader. She is warm and welcoming and she is always well-dressed. I had chosen to be a part of her networking group because she and a few other strong business women were in the group.

Rose was kind to me and interested in seeing me do well, so she offered some advice, which I accepted gratefully. She offered to go shopping with me to get new clothes. You see, I was still in "mommy mode." My clothes were appropriate for being outdoors at the park, walking kids to school, or going camping, but they were not right for business. I was very "shlumpy." Rose and I were just acquaintances at that time, so her offer was very surprising. I was honoured that this stylish, professional lawyer would take the time to shop with me. She put a couple of conditions on our shopping trip: I was not allowed to buy anything black, and I had to try on everything, even if I thought it was ugly or not my style.

Think about these conditions: they were very important because they were designed to open my eyes to "the new" and to show me what else was available to me. I had worn a lot of black, and everything I owned was comfy — jeans and T-shirts, and other super casual items.

If all I tried on were the same clothes as what I had been wearing, I would look the same as I had always looked. I had to get out of my comfort zone and try on things I thought looked disgusting, weird, or "not me." In the end, Rose and I didn't actually make it out for a shopping date. But her offer to take me shopping changed my way of thinking. I was so ready to make a change that I was willing to make mistakes. She gave me some solutions and instructions on what to do to upgrade my style, so there was little risk of failure.

When someone offers to help you, take them up on their offer. The offer itself might be all you need to solve your problem. I went out shopping and made some daring choices. The new items didn't look like me, of course: I had never worn anything like them. But they *could* be me if I changed, and I did. What I found, as I experimented with my own personal style, was that sometimes the things I thought would look disgusting on me actually looked amazing. I really had no reference points from which to make judgements or embark upon discussions. I didn't know good from bad, stylish from dumpy, my style from someone else's style. I had to start by trying it on.

The same goes for learning about your areas of greatest talent, what you love to do, who you love to spend your time with, and when, and where you will be most powerful. Sometimes we just have to try something on and make mistakes. We will err and then we will correct and make it right, and then make it even better.

When I started BLITZ Business Success I decided to get a coaching certification so that I would have additional tools to help my clients. The training program I took also taught participants how to set up and run a coaching business.

Although I was not technically running a coaching business I decided to "try on" the program model. As I mentioned earlier, I offered three-month and six-month programs. In the beginning I was terribly disappointed with the results my clients where getting. It didn't matter whether they worked with me for three months or six, they were never truly successful, and it was frustrating for me and them.

What I later discovered was that I could move people closer to their goals in a single day than I could in a six-month program. So, I tried a strategy day model. People ended up getting results faster, I was more confident of my value, and I was more successful at what I could accomplish in my business. There would be no way for me to make this statement if I had not "tried on" the coaching model first. The strategy day has become an integral part of how I work with people. When someone asks me if they can just hire me for an hour, or if they can book a couple of calls over a month, I confidently turn them down. And I offer them a VIP Day. I know that this is of greater service to both of us than if I take on every possible sale. I have more credibility and my clients get better results.

By the way, Rose and I have become good friends. We've traveled-networked together, supported each other with business, and sometimes even shopped together. If I 'd turned down her initial offer, and been unwilling to make changes and mistakes, I'd have risked more than a few mistakes, I'd have lost the chance to gain a good friend and business confidant.

Wrap-up (Part I)

Learning is a life-long process and starting a business has a large learning curve. Put in the effort up-front to learn as much as you can about how your business will work. Make sure you know and understand the basics. This is the key to becoming an Entrepreneur. Understanding the foundational pieces, the work, when to use them, etc., is the basis for a mentality you can grow.

Go back to the section on the Basics if you have not yet created your plan.

If defining your niche target market, your business brand, and your goals is not something you can do for yourself, then hire a professional to help you get it done.

With your basics in place, and an understanding of what your new mindset looks like, you can take on change while accepting that you will make mistakes. You will be ready for the transformation of the Entrepreneurial Awakening.

> *"Life is short so you need to love what you do, because you're going to do it for a long time! This 'Runway of Life' we are on has a beginning, a middle and an end – how we live it is totally up to us. Are you excited? Passionate? Turned on by your business?*
> *This new book, Entrepreneur Awakening is perfect for your runway of life. I recommend you buy it, read it and apply the philosophy to your business and your life. You might fall in love all over again. "*
> **- Dr. Peter Legge**, O.B.C., CSP, CPAE, HoF

Part II: Implement It

> *Every significant accomplishment begins with one person stepping up and committing to making a difference.*
>
> **- John C. Maxwell**

The motivation to take action and do the work is abundant when an idea is new and fresh. The excitement of starting something new and creating a dream can propel us forward to develop a plan with a deadline that is likely enthusiastically under-estimated.

Daniel Kahneman is a psychologist and statistics champion, and his book, *Thinking, Fast and Slow*, shares some excellent research. Part of it demonstrates that we are more likely to expect to succeed in a new business venture than ever accept that we might be among the 65% of all new businesses that will fail before the five-year mark.

What makes the 35% different, and why do 100% of us believe we will be among them? Kahneman refers to this as the "Planning Fallacy," and we are all susceptible. By this he means that we are likely to overestimate our level of success and underestimate the time it will take us to complete our plan. What he doesn't point out, and what I know to be true is, that without this type of "over enthusiasm" nobody would ever succeed because in order to succeed you must believe you can.

Implementing when you are excited about your vision is easier than creating your new procedures, training a new employee for the hundredth time, or making your 10 sales calls every day, four days in a row. Making your bill payments, marketing consistently, updating the bookkeeping, and other mundane business operations are uninspiring. Implementation will not be as easy, nor as high on your priority list, without an extraordinary effort to create something different. After all, it will likely take you from three to five years to become consistently profitable, if you make it at all.

We can make our estimates more accurate and our plans more valuable when we know the pitfalls we might face, one of which is a lack of motivation. So as our plan matures, and our business becomes more routine, how do we continue to motivate ourselves with the excitement and energy of a new business owner?

How do we stay on track, avoid distractions, go beyond our current limitations and beliefs, get comfortable with feeling uncomfortable, and continually look for growth opportunities?

In Part II of this book I'm going to talk about what it takes to stay on track and be successful enough to make it through the first five years and beyond in business.

Chapter 6: Take Action

The lack of desire is the reason people do not take action
- Zig Ziglar

In the book *The Secret* we are shown that we need to have focused intention to get what we want. By asking the Universe (or God, if you like) for what we want, we set our future in motion. Life is full of abundance and no one is deprived when we are the recipients of lavish prosperity. What that book does not make clear to many, however, is that we still have to do the work. You must take action.

There are three things I see when it comes to inaction:

1. Lack of understanding

2. Lack of desire

3. Procrastination

Your Plan

When opportunity presents itself. it does not hang around for an eternity waiting until someone does something. Opportunity has a shelf life and if you wait, the idea may not be fresh enough to still be a viable option. For example, have you ever been watching an "As seen on TV" commercial and recognized a product that was almost exactly the same as an idea you had some time in the past? Did you feel a little betrayed that someone else was making money off your idea?

When I was a kid my family use to play a game we called "Dictionary." One day the board game "Balderdash" came out and it was identical to our family game of "Dictionary." I couldn't believe that someone was making money off my family's game!

Of course, they made money off this game — and so they should, they deserved to. They were the ones who took the action and the risk. When I met the co-inventor, Laura Robinson, some years later, and heard her story of risk and struggle, I realized why so many people don't do the work.

Taking action when the path is not clear is very difficult work. For an employee wanting to start a business, there is an overarching incentive to stay employed because the pleasure of a regular paycheque outweighs the pain of the uncertain cost and potential for loss that is tied to launching a company. Even with a clear vision of the potential gain, the motivation to start is reduced or even absent when the path to taking action is unclear. You must understand where you want to go and, at the very least, be very clear on the first few steps you need to take to get there.

Many entrepreneurs' stories on how they got started are a result of a fundamental change in their employment. They were dismissed, downsized, or given a pay reduction. They received an unwanted early retirement or demotion, or the corporation changed and they didn't enjoy working there any longer. Whatever the circumstances of this change, they were given the opportunity to start something new, and this made the choice to start the business easier. It was the nudge they needed to put more effort into finding their next steps.

My own journey had a start-stop-start beginning. The company I worked for downsized and I was laid-off. I sought out programs to help me start a business and attended several business training sessions, as well as a grant-funded intake week for a program offered through the Canadian and Provincial governments.

I was committed and excited to begin...until an offer came in for me to work at what seemed like the perfect job: part-time work for fulltime pay at a high-tech medical device company. I had worked with several of the people at the company in the past and I loved working with them.

The company was new and aggressively moving up. Three months later I was out of a job again, the result of a poor fit between me and the company; we parted ways. I will talk about hiring great people that are a fit for your company later in the section called "The Big Biz ($1,000,000) – aka Leverage," but for now, understand that this parting allowed me to start the work of creating my companies.

I went back to the pursuit of self-employment again. I was accepted into the Self Employment Benefits program based on my business plan, and I received funding and support. I was now in action with a plan, with funding, and with the support I needed to have a great start.

Your Desire Statement

Ask yourself these two questions:

1. Do I know why I am starting this business?
2. What is my desired outcome? (AKA what do I want from this business? What's in it for me?)

Success requires you have a clear vision of your final destination and a clear understanding of why you want to get there. You can only define your path when you know where you expect to be when you finish the journey.

It's hard to book a flight if you don't know your departure and arrival locations. It's the same for business; it's hard to create a plan if you don't know what your starting point is or what your endpoint looks like.

When people first start a business, their goal is often to replace the income they had as an employee. Creating a successful business takes a much more focused vision. I talked about creating your plan in the chapter about "The Basics." Before your plan you must discover your desire.

When I read the book *Think and Grow Rich* by Napoleon Hill, I could not read past Chapter Two on Desire until I had created my own desire statement. I had never written a desire statement and I found it hard to believe it was going to make a huge difference in my business. I used the structure recommended in the book and followed the instructions for use, and I found it did make a huge difference. Here is my first desire statement.

My Desire Statement

By the first day of March, 2013, I will have in my hand the value of $10,000 or more for one large speaking engagement plus several thousands of dollars in my account from smaller engagements booked over the previous four months. In return for this money I will give talks filled with passion and love that move the audiences to action and emotional learning in the capacity as speaker of business and life success. I believe I will have this money in my possession. My faith is so strong I can now see this cheque and my overflowing bank statement before my eyes. I can feel it with my hands.

It is now waiting delivery to me in the amount and currency I requested at the time I deliver the service I will provide for it.

I am awaiting a plan in which to receive this money and I will follow that plan when it is received.

I created a vision that was so clear to my unconscious that it knew it was true. I focused on my desire statement daily, which ensured that my conscious and my subconscious minds were both working constantly on my vision. The next thing that happened was amazing.

I ended up with 17 speaking engagements in the eight months between the time I wrote this and the time it became real, including a weekly TV show of which I was the business expert and host.

I was also awarded a teaching position at my local college where I taught a course in Introduction to Entrepreneurship. The TV opportunity alone gave me an additional 62 chances to be in front of an audience.

Each item in my vision started coming true. Opportunities to make it real fell right into my lap, or so it seemed. I started saying yes more often.

I started getting more connections, more help, more clients, and more money. Finally, the entire statement had been realized about three months after the date I had written it.

I want this for you, too, so I am including the instructions on how to create your own desire statement in the resource chapter at the end of this book, but don't go there yet because I want to show you the pitfall of this statement as it was written in *Think and Grow Rich*.

The Pitfall

After this first flush of success, I continued to use the desire statement but I did not continue to get what I asked for.

It was not until 2015, when I reread *Think and Grow Rich* that I recognized a contradiction with the process Napoleon Hill describes and what he actually did. It is subtle, yet it is a powerful distinction for success.

In *Think and Grow Rich* the first step to creating your Desire Statement states, "Be definite as to the amount." It clearly, and in no uncertain terms, instructs the reader to "fix it in your mind the exact amount of money you desire."

As I read through the book I realized that all the examples Mr. Hill had already cited did not do this. They did not list the dollar amount. They were not looking for an exact amount of cash. It was NOT all about the MONEY!

In fact, as I continued to read the book I realized it was NEVER about the MONEY. So, what was it really about? It was about their greatest desires – The Outcome – The thing that engaged them, would change their lives, would make a difference, would align with their beliefs about life and people. Here are three examples directly from the book.

- Napoleon Hill's own desire was focused on his son, born without ears. He had decided that he would do everything to ensure that his son would hear and speak, and he did, in an era when the technology and science had not yet discovered these possibilities. ("A Desire Backed By Faith.")

- A tenant's daughter was sent by her mother to get 50 cents from a mill owner. With great risk to her own health and potentially her life, she stood her ground against a grown man to get what she came for. She was driven by the desire to obey her mother, not the desire to obtain 50 cents. ("A Desire to Obey.")

- Edwin C. Barnes' desire was to "become the business associate of a great inventor," not to make money as an inventor working with Thomas A. Edison. It was his consuming obsession and he was going to see his desire accomplished or "perish." ("A Desire to contributed and belong.")

This does not exclude money as the possible focus of your own statement, of course. If your desired outcome is to create money, then it is the right statement.

This now made more sense to me. The money never felt aligned with my view on what I wanted to do. My smart friends who are money experts teach that "Money is not real."

If this is true, then why am I desiring something that is not real? And if it is not real, then what is?

In the book *The Bhagavad Gita*[6], the teachings state that the only thing that is real is that which does not change.

So, what about me and my purpose and passion does not change? What about you does not change? I can tell you it is not money.

As your life changes your needs change and the requirement for money changes. I know that when I was traveling around Australia in my early 20s I did not need much money. I would stay with new friends, eat or not eat, depending on my needs, work where I could, and I generally focused on enjoying the experience.

Now that I have kids and I make significantly more money than I did when I was traveling, I need different things, not just for myself, but for my family.

What has not changed is my desire to stay with friends, eat, and enjoy the experience.

I've learned that the thread that is woven through all of my experiences is my desire to teach and share what I've learned.

When I was a child, adults would say, "Barb is so mature for a four-year-old — ask her to help." In public school, I would help my classmates when the teacher was absent.

And, as an adult, I actually teach college students, helping them to learn and understand. This is a theme in my life.

What is your theme and how does it align with your true desire?

---

[6] The Bhagavad Gita, translated by Eknath Easwaran

Here is a later desire statement. Observe how it is subtly different than the first one I created.

> *By June 2016 I will have completed the first year of an advisory board designed to support the accelerated growth, profitability, and sustainability of six-figure businesses and I will have put in place support from experts for the members. In return for their membership, business owners will receive powerful growth development days, plans to follow and implement, and they will experience measurable growth to meet and exceed their goals. I will be fully committed to the success of the members and the board coordinators' businesses. I will work to change the overall success of small business in Canada and around the world. Small six-figure business owners will eagerly and easily pay to take part in this program.*
> *I will use the results of the first board to market others. I will provide a high-level, fully-managed experience of comfort and excellence, and I will add online experiences, more peer connections and professional locations. I will share my own inner circle of experts with members. I will work towards adding future retreats, boards in other provinces, and a conference.*
> *My vision is to create a Canadian corporation that can provide employment and business opportunities for people around the world.*

As a result of this desire statement the first advisory board saw 100% of the members meet or exceed their goals for that year. I can tell you, I was even skeptical at first when one of the member's goal was to increase their sales by 50% over the year previous.

It was really miraculous to see them work at their businesses, no harder than the year before, with the result that they increased their sales by 95%, well beyond their expectations. My desire statement benefited everyone.

Staying Motivated

The third challenge around taking action is procrastination. It is incredibly difficult to accomplish anything if you only think about and plan on doing the work. You must take action.

Know Your Goal

You must review your top goals regularly. You must have an emotional connection to their completion. If your top goal is written as "make more money," it will not be as impactful or compelling to your motivation as "having $25,000 for a down-payment on a house by the end of the year." I am going to talk about SMARTAR[7] goals later in this section because understanding how to create goals is really important in completing tasks. In fact, having something in your life that you really want to complete is extremely important for your motivation, too, and I will continue to mention goals throughout this book. With more motivation, you will be driven to see more opportunities, learn more ways to succeed, and implement more of your plan in a timely manner. And in many cases, it will help you side-step unforeseen challenges as they arise.

Understand the Path

It's much easier to be motivated when you've something to do that you know you can accomplish. Make your daily tasks something you can complete. Keep the list short and ask yourself if each task will get you closer to your goal. It sounds easy, but managing the routing of working IN and ON your business will make this less likely to happen. If you can make it a routine by setting your "to do" list at the end of the day for the next day, or reviewing your "to do" list at the beginning of every day, you will increase your chances of completing the tasks and moving closer to completing your plan.

---

[7] See my article on this goal setting process at http://bit.ly/SMARTAR

Accomplishments

Don't gloss over your accomplishments. You must spend time feeling grateful for the tasks you have finished, the deadline you have met, the sales you have made, the people you have helped, and the goals you have completed.

Even recognizing the value of a failure will help you learn quicker and move on. Inspire yourself with your own accomplishments so you can continue to push forward and create a successful and profitable business.

Taking action in your business can be hard some days. Laundry, kids, self-pity, and life experiences can sneak in and steal your resolve to make something great.

If you start your day with your plan and your to-do list, and end your day with a review of what you have accomplished, you will be completing more work and getting closer to your goals every day.

Review

To take action, do these three things:

1. Have a plan that allows you to easily understand your next steps

2. Know your desired income.

3. Have a "to do" list each day focused on completing your goals.

4. Celebrate your accomplishments.

Bonus - Have an accountability partner to help you stay focused so you can avoid procrastination.

Focusing on your desire and staying on course will help you stay in action, reach your target, and make bigger things happen.

Chapter 7: Bright Shiny Object Syndrome (BSOS)

> Most people think that intelligence is about brain, where really it's about focus. Genius is just attention to a subject until it becomes specific, specific, specific.
> **- Abraham Hicks**

Start a business — write a book — sell VoIP phone systems — become a director — investigate a new product patent — attend a trade show — manage a contractor in a project — do the work. These are some of the things I had on my plate at one point, a few years back.

There is always plenty to do when running your own business, but adding new projects without successfully completing the current ones can fracture your focus and slow your progression, as well as interfere with deadlines. If the deadlines are for your client, it can result in lost revenue and reduced growth.

"Bright Shiny Object Syndrome," or BSOS, describes a level of distraction that is not beneficial to the growth of the business. Doing too much at once and then taking on something that is not part of your core goal is like a shiny object that catches your attention and draws your gaze away from your current focus.

What is your core task?

You must know the answer to this question if you want to have intentional growth in your business. It is tied to your desired outcome, your set goals, and your daily "to do" list. It is part of your plan and it's the next step of implementation that allows you to systematically create the new components of your business.

Business Need

When starting a business, it is understood that you will need a business card. Sometimes new business owners will not create a business card until they have completed their brand and perfected their image. Their plan may look like this:

1. Develop Brand

2. Decide on Name

3. Create Logo

4. Design Website

5. Get Business Phone Number

6. Design Cards

7. Print cards

The problem with this linear thinking is that this person may refrain from doing any business because they feel incapable of portraying a professional image without their card or website. In this list, there is a lot of room for procrastination.

For instance, below is a list of other additional work (procrastination work) that may have come out of some of the original steps above, derailing the timeline and lengthening the time it takes to actually get out there and start.

These are "**sub-steps**" to some (1, 3, 4, 5, 7) of the steps in the plans described above:

1. Develop Brand

    a. Create value and mission statements

2. Decide on Name

3. Create Logo

    a. Play around with graphic software to learn how to create a logo.

4. Design Website

    a. Learn HTML

    b. Learn social media and set up profiles

5. Get Business Phone Number

    a. Investigate new phone systems and technology

6. Design Cards

7. Print cards

    a. Evaluate printers to save on printing costs

These are all shiny objects, new processes, and distractions to keep you busy doing things that are not revenue-generating activities. After all, people who are wed to this model cannot generate revenue by reaching out to any new clients until they complete what they need to do first (get a business card, website, or a business phone number). For small business owners, success often starts with the simple determination to just get started.

Being distracted by "the new" is a way to avoid something that must get done. Here are two ways to stay on track so you can identify when you are being distracted by a bright shiny object and not growing your business.

1. Know Your Big Goals
You should have set a few big goals to reach in the next six-to-12 months. For example, maybe you need to break-even in 12 months.

[The break-even point in a business is when the money coming in equals the money going out
(Income = Expenses)]

To break even, you may have determined that you need five new clients a month and so far you are only averaging two new clients for every 15 prospects you talk to. That means you need to talk to 75 prospects a month to reach your goal of five new clients. By month 12 you need to have a sales funnel that allows you to talk to 75 prospects each month.

To define your own big goals, I recommend that you use the SMARTAR rules system to help create goals that you can accomplish. SMARTAR is a compilation of the SMART goals, which are taught in most business programs, plus my additional "AR" components to help ensure you're getting adequate encouragement around your goals in order to complete them.

The SMART in the **SMART**AR acronym stands for:

S = Specific

M = Measurable

A = Achievable

R = Realistic

T = Time-bound

This concept is taught in numerous places and courses so I will not go into it here.

The additional "AR" in the SMART**AR** acronym stands for:

A = Action with Accountability

You must take action. If you have made a plan for what must be done, then stick to it.

The best way to complete something is to tell someone else you are going to do it. You know that the next time you see them they are going to ask how the task is going. You also know you cannot avoid them forever (unless you tell a stranger, but that doesn't count). Being accountable to another person will propel you faster towards your goals.

R = Risk and Reward

You will be taking a risk when you tell another person about your goals. The risks range from someone stealing your ideas, or laughing at you, or labelling you a dreamer. The risk of *not* making a goal is that you will never reach your destination. It truly is only a dream if you have not set a goal and made it SMART.

So, you have taken a risk and set your goals, used the SMART rules to define the goals and then taken action with accountability. One thing many people forget to do when they reach a goal is to reward themselves for all the effort it took to get to the finish line. Some would say the goal itself is the reward, but I believe that when we stop to celebrate the action and commitment we start to recognize what we are really capable of doing. So, tell yourself when you set a goal what your reward will be. Make it something great so you will celebrate when you've completed the work and reach your goal.

2. Know Your Daily Tasks
I believe that it is important to set daily tasks. Choose three tasks that will help you reach your goals and an additional one-to-three tasks that are administrative in nature. The admin work simply has to get done. These tasks may include things like: banking, purchasing supplies, or backing up your computer. You cannot ignore these, but if you make your daily "to do" list full of admin work, you will not get closer to your goals.

The tasks that get you to your goals may not be as easy to define. In our example of reaching the break-even point aon previous page, it was determined the person needed to talk to 75 prospects per month. There's a step missing here that relates to the interim goals involved in reaching your big goal. In this example, the business owner cannot just contact 75 people, she needs to know how to pull them in, interact with them and engage them. She has to continually fill her sales funnel with new prospects so she has someone to sell to each month.

Maybe she can pull them in by meeting with them in person. If so, where will she find a large concentration of these potential clients? Once she knows that, she can attend the meetings, speak at an event, or pay for advertising, and that will put her in front of them.

Maybe she can interact with them in a seminar or webinar. If so, how will she get them to attend? Once she knows the steps to attract them to her webinars, she will need to perform those steps regularly.

Maybe she can engage the potential clients on social media, through a newsletter, or on the phone? These are all very different technologies and take different skills to implement and maintain. Knowing that she needs these skills may require training, or possibly the hiring of a contractor.

After she knows how to reach her clients, our entrepreneur can focus on her sales conversations and then create her daily task list. For example, it may look like this:

Monday

- Call five prospects
- Engage in social media (Facebook and Twitter)
- Go to a BNI meeting

Tuesday

- Write an article for the newsletter
- Call five prospects
- Have a meeting with a prospect

Wednesday

- Etc.

Do the work every day. In this example, if our business owner could make five calls each day, she would meet her monthly requirement of contacting 75 people in just three weeks, and potentially become profitable (Income > Expenses) in that month. The challenge will be to keep the phone list filled so she can have five people to call every day.

3. Self-Diagnosis

Things that are not on your daily task list and are not revenue-generating activities, or part of your big goal, are outside of your daily scope and are likely a distraction. You may have BSOS. If you find that you are not completing your daily tasks, and you are often distracted, you are likely prone to BSOS. Try taking a break when you notice that you are off task. Then re-evaluate your daily tasks and restart.

When we were talking about the person who needed business cards in the BSOS section, the goal was really not defined. The goal was not to create a business card but to be able to connect with a prospect. With the knowledge of the big goal, the steps could look like this:

a) Get a business phone number

b) Print a simple name card

c) Put up a single webpage with your contact info

d) Start sharing what you offer

e) Develop your brand

f) Decide on your business name

g) Create your logo

h) Design your website

i) Design your official cards

j) Print your business cards

Note that the first three items are quick implementation tasks to help this person get right to their revenue generating activities. Now they can start networking, inviting people to meetings, and making calls while they are building their brand.

It will also be more difficult for them to be distracted by bright shiny objects because they will be focused on revenue-generating activities infused with planned business development activities.

> *"Thank you for a great read! I especially loved chapter 8 "Think Big." Your style is clear and easy to understand. I learned a lot ... extremely insightful."*
> **- Denise O'Brien**

Chapter 8: Think Big

You playing small doesn't serve the world. There's nothing enlightening about shrinking so that others won't feel uncomfortable around you. As you let your own light shine, you indirectly give others permission to do the same.
- Marianne Williamson

To "Think Big" we must go beyond our current limitations and beliefs.

When I'm teaching about building a business I always have my clients refer to their big picture business.

If you want to have a business of a certain size you must know how to build a business at least 10 times as big. I call this my 10x Rule. By doing this you are simply preparing for the inevitable: Successful Growth!

Many employees get into business and only look to replace their wage or make a certain amount of money more than that amount. They build a business that creates that exact wage and then two things can and will happen:

1. They cannot make that wage because as soon as they get close they have to stop seeking new business for fear of not being able to handle more.

2. They get more business than they are prepared to handle and they start missing deadlines; then their product or service deteriorates.

If you do not know what the next step is after your last step is achieved, there is nowhere to go but down. Let's use an example of a make-believe business owner named Maggie. Maggie's "Big Picture Business" is not extravagant.

She wants to build a modest business that has a yearly income of $100,000. By the 10x Rule I referred to above, she should be looking at what it takes to build a business of $1,000,000. Let's look at the numbers and required resources to see why this is true; but first I want to define "Time Types."

Time Types

There are two types of time a CEO puts in their business:

The first Time Type is billable time. This is the time spent working on the client's project or service delivery. In massage therapy, it is the time spent giving the client a massage. In my first company, it was the time I spent writing documents, and designing manuals, or help-systems. It was the time I could charge to the client.

The second Time Type is your CEO time. This is the work of the business. This is paid by your company and is not billable. CEO time is spent managing your contractors, paying bills, networking, writing marketing copy, answering emails, making sales calls, being the visionary, etc. When your business is just you, your CEO Time is everything that is not billable hours.

The Small Biz ($100,000)

Maggie wants a small business that employs only her. Her target revenue is $100,000 per year. She needs to start by understanding her pricing model. Let's say she offers three services:

1. 1 hour of consulting @ $95

2. A 10-hour package @ $950

3. An intake package at $250 for 2.5 hours

In general, a business owner should not allocate more than 20 hours/week to billable time. The other time is used for marketing, operations, and admin work.

If Maggie sold only the 10-hour package, she would have to work 22 hours/week for 50 weeks to make her $100,000. This is doable but, as you can see, she is already starting to chip into her CEO Time.

As the CEO Time is reduced and the billable hours go up, the business owner cannot do the work of the business and will start experiencing a financial rollercoaster. If you do little or no marketing while you work on a client's project, then you will have no new clients when the project is done. Because of this, a business owner will work like crazy to get new clients while there is no money coming in and the cycle will start again.

This is a stressful way to run a business and there is no guarantee that you will be compensated when there are no projects. This type of struggle can reduce the confidence of talented people and may further exacerbate the unbalanced lifestyle it creates.

The key to a more balanced income and work-life is to always have new clients coming into the funnel and always have new projects starting.

This means the marketing must always get done, regularly and consistently. To do this, the CEO Time must be maintained. If there is too much work to allow for the CEO Time, then work must be offloaded to others or streamlined using systems and automation.

Offloading work means hiring, and, to a business owner with an employee mindset, this is stressful, especially when the business plan shows the owner as the only employee. Their first thought is often, "how can I afford to hire a full- or part-time person?"

As long as Maggie is unwilling to at least prepare for a larger business, she will always be riding the rollercoaster of financial instability.

A Story About Leverage

My friend and fellow business owner Cathy (not her real name) had a challenge around her CEO Time. She had been a successful sales rep for a women's clothing designer for years but she had developed some executive coaching programs for women that she wanted to deliver full-time. Cathy is organized and prepared for her clients. Her home was clean and orderly, as she needs the "white space," both physically and emotionally, to be able to create and sell. Her home office, on the other hand, was a dumping zone for everything in her home that didn't have a permanent place.

Filing was a chore and Cathy hated it so much that she would procrastinate on clearing her space. She regularly worked with a virtual assistant, but they could offer no in-office support for Cathy. Her untidy desk stopped her from making sales calls, a critical task. Without new sales, her coaching business was not generating new clients. Without new coaching clients, she was required to sell more clothes, and that meant more time on the road and at clients' homes showing her product. This was not the growth she had imagined. She had envisioned a business based 100% on coaching with no clothing sales at all, and she was living an opposite reality. Changes in her business growth were tied to the administration work of her CEO Time, which she could not successfully complete.

When Cathy and I discussed her situation, we discovered that her admin work did not require any specialized knowledge or training. So, next we started looking for someone she could hire who did not require any specialized training and who would be willing to work a few hours a week. The answer was the neighbour's teenage daughter, who was a student at the time. For about $10 an hour the young girl could come in for two hours every week to file and tidy. This represented two extra hours of free time that would allow Cathy to focus on marketing. This would free her from the procrastination that was costing her so dearly. The new client work would cover more than 10x what Cathy was paying the student weekly.

And that is exactly the path that Cathy followed.

> *About a year later she was able to completely let go of the clothing sales side of her business to focus entirely on her coaching. She still makes great money, she does what she loves, and she has time for her family. She now feels she has a successful business in which she loves to work.*
>
> *This situation shows us that it is not easy to maintain a small business doing what we expect to do without a plan to be able to handle more work than we expect. I believe that this is one of the reasons that so many small businesses fail in the first five years.*

The Big Biz ($1,000,000) – aka Leverage

> *Big businesses do not get bigger by shuffling what they know, and doing the same thing over and over. Big businesses get bigger with investment in the business and its leaders, so they can do new things and create new opportunities.*
> *- **Barb Stuhlemmer***

When a business owner spends time discovering what it will take to create a 10x business, she understands so much more about what can go wrong and how to handle it.

Some roles will require additional support at different stages of a business's growth, and if a business owner can anticipate these needs they will be able to manage more projects and help maintain income consistency.

Let's go back to the example of Maggie the consultant. If Maggie wants the small business model to be successful, she needs to understand what is required for a big business. This is her 10x business strategy.

To determine a 10x strategy for this business, let's look back at the numbers we imagined earlier. Remember that each of these products is a one-to-one service.

So, if Maggie sells a 10-hour program, she has to have 10 hours available in which to deliver that program.

Here, again, is Maggie's pricing model:

1. 1 hour of consulting time @ $95

2. A 10-hour package @ $950

3. An Intake package at $250 for 2.5 hours

Obviously, Maggie needs to be able to leverage her time. We know that with these numbers she cannot hit the $100,000 mark without eating into her CEO time.

Maggie can leverage time in her business in one of three ways:

- Serve more people (leverage space)

- Add systems and automate (leverage efficiencies)

- Hire someone (leverage time)

Let's look at these in more detail:

Serve More People

Creating a product or service that will serve many people instead of just one will immediately have several benefits. It:

a) gives clients more access for less money

b) gets Maggie more income for less time

c) creates instant growth

Maggie's clients can get access to Maggie without paying $95 an hour. Maggie could create a 10-week group program (1 hour per week) for which 10 people could pay $500 each. Maggie makes $5,000 for the delivery of this program and each person gets to work with Maggie for more than twice the amount of time they would have received in the one-to-one model of the same price.

If Maggie has products to sell, she can offer them to a larger market, in new locations, or even online. By reaching more clients, she could reduce the price slightly as an introduction to a new market. What would you rather do: sell 10 products at $10 each or get 20 new clients by selling your product at $8.50 as an introductory price?

> [WARNING] Be careful about basing your sales model on offering the "lowest price." If you sell your products as the lowest price in their niche, you will always be fighting this war and eventually someone will sell at a price that is lower than yours. Clients who are attracted to items that sell for the lowest price do not have the same loyalty as those who are willing to pay more for greater value. Use a discount for initial market penetration or as a "sale."

New sales to new clients always mean growth for your business as it is easier to sell again to a past client than it is to get a new client.

For product-based sales, leverage can also be created through the sale of packages or promotions. These allow the business owner to provide bonus products or discounts for multiple sales.
Here are some examples you will probably recognize:
- Buy two get one free
- BOGO
- Baker's Dozen
- Spend $100 and get 10% off

Systems and Automation

Finding a way to offer a service by working more efficiently, or without using any of your time at all, is key to creating leverage with systems and automation. This may be more obvious in a manufacturing business than a service-based business.

Making something by hand and creating a one-off product is more time consuming than automating the process and creating 10 or 100 of the product per hour. One-offs are worth more money but require more effort to sell, and more time to make.

In service, automation may best be used in the delivery of your service. Now that Maggie, our example entrepreneur, has created a 10-week group program, and she is serving more people, she can add automation to further reduce the amount of time it takes to maintain the relationship and deliver on her promises. Here's how she can do that:

> **Step 1.** Deliver the 10-week program and record it at the time of the first delivery.

> **Step 2.** Sell the recorded program as an additional product

> **Step 3.** Use an online shopping cart system to automate the sign up, payments, messaging, and delivery of the recordings.

> **Step 4.** BONUS value: Add an additional group call (e.g. +2 hours) to the recorded program (0 hours) to add some personal connection, which helps with sales and your clients' learning.

Maggie has just created an online program that delivers 12 hours of training but can be delivered using only two hours of her time. Except for the group call, it requires none of her time to get payments, deliver the product, or give instructions to her clients. She only had to create it once, and then support it with a single group call.

What does this mean for your bottom line?

- You can sell your recorded program with live support for less of your time and even less cost to your clients... and still deliver value.

- Your clients can benefit from your expertise without having to pay the big-ticket price.

- You have the opportunity to sell just the recording with unlimited downloads and no additional time required, ever.

- You can add your recorded program as a bonus to other programs, increasing their value and other sales.

I hope you get a sense of how lucrative this could be. Recently I learned of a membership site that had 20,000 members who paid $7 per month for their membership. Every aspect of this service involves leveraged time and almost everything is automated. The owners are making $140,000 per month to create the valuable content, manage the system, and handle the memberships. The only true work each month revolves around creating the new content; everything else is automated.

Hire

If you need to do more of your core work and less of the work you are not best at doing, then you need to hire. Whether it is full-time, part-time, contract, project based, or bartered time, getting someone to do the work that does not represent the best use of your time will free you to grow your business. It is likely that your business cannot ever get to the $100,000 mark without hiring someone to help with specific tasks.

Your new hires should do one of two things for you:

1. Free you up so you can make more money, or

2. Make you more money

Someone who does your bookkeeping or admin work is not making sales or looking after your clients. How are they helping the company, and you, make more money? By freeing you from that chore so you can focus on making more sales calls and delivering more service.

The challenge is to do the hiring before you actually need more employees, and grow your business because you have them. You must do the work to increase sales when you hire someone, there is no other option. As long as you are in charge of everything, you cannot make enough money to truly hire another person into your business.

A client came to me recently with the ag- old problem of "I cannot afford to hire anyone and I don't have time to do anything more in my business." This lady, let's call her Dorothy, is a successful massage therapist with a full practice of about 15-20 clients a week. She cannot take on more clients. She wanted to increase her profits, and she identified having more clients as the best way to do this. Dorothy and I started by looking at her gross income. Then we did a quick calculation of all of her general costs. Where was there room to hire more help? In the laundry. Dorothy had wanted to save on the cost of sending her laundry out for professionally cleaning and she was spending about four hours a week over six nights, doing the work herself.

When we calculated her electricity, water, and gas costs, we discovered that she was spending about $150/month to do her own laundry, which didn't take into account the cost of the 16 hours or so she was spending at the task. If she had those 16 hours in the evening to do other admin work (which she was also managing herself), she would have time during the day to take on new clients.

Dorothy had two choices:

1. 16 hours per month of her time + $150/month in home utilities.

2. No time + $300/month for the professional laundry service.

By choosing to send the laundry out, Dorothy actually has time to take on more than enough clients to make up for the increase in costs. She had created leverage in her business by knowing her numbers so she could justify the expense of hiring someone.

Now let's use this understanding of leverage to determine how much product and support would need to be sold in order to create Maggie's 10x Business of $1,000,000 per year ($83,333/month). Knowing these numbers will help her understand the path to a bigger business because she will know the trigger points for hiring. It's the same for you.

We said earlier that Maggie sells

- One hour of time @ $95

- A 10-hour package @ $950

- An intake package at $250 for 2.5 hours

To reach $83,333 per month Maggie must:

1. Work 877 hours/month @$95/hour OR

2. Make 92 sales of her 10-hour package @$900 and work 920 hours/month OR

3. Make 333 sales of her $250/2.5 hour product and work 833 hours/month OR

4. Make 416 sales and work 416 hours/month @$200/hour if she simply increased her fee to $200/hour.

Again, remember that each of Maggie's packages are delivered as a one-to-one service, meaning that she must have 10 hours for each person that purchases her $900 package.

The average person works about 160 – 200 hours per month, which means that even if Maggie sold her newly-priced product at $200/hour (more than Maggie's current price) she would need more than two people to deliver the work.

Without leverage, a million dollar business is not even an option for Maggie's business, or for any solo-preneur with similar services and pricing and support. It is simply not physically possible.

Start asking these questions to get an idea of what you will need in your 10x business to ensure you are capable of giving your clients great service and quality experiences with your company:

- Which product will I likely sell most?
- How many people will I need managing all the hours required to deliver the product I expect to sell?
- Which skill sets will I need to add to my employee base?
- Which roles (responsibilities) will I still complete myself?
- What technology will I need in order to support my people?
- What space will I need?
- How will my marketing change?
- What other support will I need for my people (regulations, employment resources, training, etc.)?

Smaller businesses that understand what is needed for the 10x business will be better able to plan ahead.

I have found that as my company grows I have been able to hire in time, just before there would be a crippling need for more support.

Hiring when you are already overwhelmed takes more time, and costs more money, than planning ahead, and it will likely require more effort to get the right person in the appropriate positions. Believe me when I say that this path also has more stress.

When you reach the limits of your small business (the $100,000 business) you are very likely to stop taking on new clients if you do not know what the business will look like and who is supporting it at $150,000 / $250,000 / $500,000 etc.

Evaluating the 10x business model will eliminate surprises and reduce the challenges that come when you get several clients at the same time. Income levels will even out and your clients will be more likely to come back, because they know you can serve them, no matter how many other clients you currently have.

Now that Maggie knows what it would take to manage a $1,000,000 business she has a much better idea of what she can do when she gets close to $100,000.

For example, let's say she has three proposals out. Before she understood her 10x business rule she would think, "If I get contract A and B I will have to turn down contract C." Now that she has evaluated contractors and is ready for the possibility of growth, she can accept all three contracts and still manage her own CEO work so that her sales funnel is never empty.

Knowing your bigger business transition levels, and knowing when to hire, will help you feel less overwhelmed.

Growth will feel doable and you will still find it easier to say "yes" to the work. You will land more clients when you have this confidence because you know how to handle the additional work.

DREAM the dreams and know you can make them POSSIBLE!

"The most useful part in Chapter 8 describes the cycle of work with no marketing work done, then no work, marketing done, then work but no marketing, then no work etc.- and what to do about it. I am going to dedicate a half-day per week to start and get some Facebook and website content going and try to create some routines so that these messages are going out on a regular basis whether we are working or not. The "CEO time" was very well explained and my husband, who is a voice-over artist, also benefitted from the concept. Hiring a bookkeeper is first on my list once we get going and the pricing ideas you gave of adding value and differentiating/finding your niche is also very useful."

- Toby MacPhee

Chapter 9: Make Decisions

I am not a product of my circumstances. I am a product of my decisions.
- Stephen Covey

"I have all the information you asked for. I've evaluated three different software packages, judged their value against what we need for the help pages, and I've compared their prices. Here is a matrix to help you see the pros and cons of each of our choices. The final choice is, of course, to do nothing and leave the product without an internal help system."

Those words were taken from a proposal I gave to my boss some years ago. As an employee I can recommend alternatives, but I don't get to decide which one is chosen.

People in management positions have more control over their budgets, but upper management and the CEO always have the final say. They define the company's direction.

A solo-preneur (self-employed) has to make big decisions about the direction of their business, and they have to give themselves permission to spend time and money on items that do not seem to have an immediate return on investment — like software, conferences, coaching, memberships, etc.

Purchasing is only one aspect of decision-making. When we are the boss, and we are the only one at the top, we evaluate and decide upon all ideas and opportunities. Clear decision-making that benefits the company's growth is a skill that must be modelled, learned, practiced and honed. A business owner needs to become an expert at this while overcoming any fear of making a bad decision that will cost money and time. Let me help you with this right now: you will make a decision in your company at some time that will ultimately cost you money and time. This is a given.

Will that cost become a great investment in the growth of your business or an expense towards your downfall? That is the question you need to be able to answer. Even bad investments can become great growth opportunities, if you look at them properly. Viewing a cost as an investment instead of a loss will help with decision-making, every time.

The Fear of Decisions

We are often afraid of making decisions because we are worried that we will make the wrong decision. And what can a wrong decision cost us? Well, when we are afraid, it feels like it can cost us our lives, relationships, home, security, and future. Often the cost is not that large, but it can be. So how do we make great decisions that actually make us money instead of losing it? Let me tell you a story about a bad decision I made about a good investment.

It looked like a great investment: For about $500 I could start a secondary business that would support my first by helping my clients get business support infrastructure at a really great price. I evaluated this opportunity and determined there were good reasons for making the investment. And I'd developed a plan for quickly recouping my money. The business I was investing in was sound: 20 years old - well established. I went ahead confidently. What I missed in my decision-making was the importance of including an evaluation of how well my available time, interest or skills would suit the opportunity. It turned out the only way to generate the bonuses to help me earn my initial investment back was to do a lot of work in this new company immediately. There was no bonus for doing the work two months later and I had not looked at this during my evaluation. I no time available to invest in this new company for at least two months. If I'd waited to invest in this opportunity, I'd have earned the bonus I needed to pay back my investment, because I would have had the time needed to create new income streams. I had failed to correctly evaluate my options and lost $500. This was a small loss, as business losses go, but not a small personal loss to my ego.

Learning when to say "Yes" is as important as knowing when to say "No." After this mistake, I was afraid people would find out how poor my judgement was.

I worried that people would believe I was not capable of understanding business value.

My business expertise was in question, at least by me. Not only was I afraid to talk about what had happened, I was afraid to make the same mistake; and so I said "no" a lot, even when I should have been saying "yes."

One mistake had made me afraid to make investment decisions and that, in itself, is a decision which does not hold any value for business growth.

Now that I have a better handle on how to evaluate opportunities well, I am no longer afraid of making decisions. It was a tough lesson to learn.

Decision-Making

Your business will require you to make big and small decisions routinely. Do I spend half an hour on Facebook for my marketing or half a day? Do I make sales calls or develop a new product? Do I enter my own sales slips or hire a bookkeeper? Do I invest in the big trade show or become a member of a weekly word-of-mouth networking group? Do I join the Chamber's board of directors or volunteer for a charity event, or both? How much time, money, or products do I give to charity or sponsorships?

There are so many things you can do to grow your business, so many ways you can spend your time and money, that it will be key for you to know how to mitigate the mistakes you will make so that they become great learning opportunities for the growth of your business, and not the cause of your business failure.

The #1 Rule of Decision Making: Know Your Plan

Have you created a business plan yet? In the chapter on "The Basics" I talked about "The Plan." If you know where you want your business to be in a year, you can use the plan to help you evaluate decisions. Using the knowledge of your 10x Rule (from the "Think Big" chapter), and your plan, you can start comparing what you will have with where you want to invest. I'm going to give you three very different examples of how decision-making works.

[A] Chairing an Advisory Board

I do a fair amount of volunteer work and because I am fairly well-known in my community I get asked to do a lot more. So much so, that one day I realized I could no longer simply say "yes" or "no," I needed a way to effectively evaluate my time.

I needed to know the value I could bring to the position and the effect it would have on my business and family life. I looked at my plan and ask these three questions:

1. Who is my ideal client?

2. How am I reaching them?

3. What are my marketing responsibilities and how much time do I have for them?

To be strategic, I decided all volunteer time connected to my business had to fit into my marketing budget for time and cost.

1. Who is my ideal client?

When I evaluate a request to volunteer I think, "Does this opportunity allow me to be in front of my ideal client? Will I be connected to the people who see my ideal client? Does this opportunity give me credibility in the eyes of my ideal client? If I answer "yes" to those questions, I move on to the next area of my business plan, and my second question.

2. How am I reaching them?

I look at my plan to identify my top three best ways to reach my clients. For me it is networking, speaking, and holding events (teaching and workshops). If a prospective volunteer position helps me get more opportunity to network, speak, or teach, then I'm doing the right thing. Now I look at my last question to evaluate my available time.

3. How much time will I set aside for marketing?

Since volunteering is tied to my marketing plan, I need to know how much time the organization is asking me to donate and how much money, if any, I have to invest.

I have found that most not-for-profits (NFP) and charities are really good at knowing exactly how much time they expect you to donate, but some have no idea. I have made a set number of hours a month available for volunteer work in my marketing. If the time they quote me fits into the time I have allocated for giving, then I say "yes." If the NFP does not know how much time the commitment would require, and I really want to give to them, then I say "yes" but qualify how much time I am willing to give.

Don't just write anyone a blank cheque for your time. You will end up regretting your choice and possibly not getting the outcome you desire for yourself or for them.

> Note – when donating your professional time (e.g. doing videos for a charity because you are a videographer) then look at getting a receipt as a "gift in kind," if your laws permit it, or send a zeroed-out invoice showing the value of your time gifted with a zero balance owning. This way you can write off your effort in your business. (See your accountant for specific tax laws that affect your business.)

> *Some other considerations:*
> *Volunteer time may also be aligned with your business and a way to connect with new clients or partners. The challenge is that your volunteer time must align with your ideas around how you want to show up and contribute in the world. Brendon Burchard in his book **The Charge** says, "Ours is a society that has falsely assumed that contributions must mean giving to some specific cause rather than simply giving of our best selves." If you are not aligned with the cause for which you are volunteering, and you are hoping to get business out of it, you will likely fail as it will feel like you are pushing. You need to be happy giving the time. Ask yourself, "Will I get to do what I love to do with the people with whom I enjoy sharing time?" If the answer is no, then don't do it.*

[B] Examining a Business Buy-in

I was once offered the opportunity to purchase another person's business. It was a micro-business that was doing well and it involved clients I would have loved to work with. I kept saying "no" because when I evaluated the opportunity, it did not align with either my personal growth plan or my happiness. Yes, I evaluate on happiness. After all, if I am going to put hours, days, weeks, or years into something, then I want to be happy with what I am doing every day, not just with my final results. Happiness with the entire process is a goal because, after all, we only have "now," and tomorrow may never come.

If my available time to invest in a business would allow me to run the business the way the last business owner ran it, but not allow me to fulfill my plans to restructure the business, then I know I would not be happy with the outcome. If my vision for growth is unmanageable because of the inadequate projected income, then I won't be happy.

And, finally, if the person selling the business has a price tag on it that is significantly more than the amount my evaluation says the company is worth, then I'm definitely not going to be happy.

Emotional purchases are not a sound way to make quick decisions. Purchasing decisions that leave you feeling emotionally interested in investing tend to fit well with the long-term effort required to build a business that you purchase.

[C] Deciding on New Equipment

When money is tight, it is easy to say "no" to large capital purchases. When your company is doing well you may make quick decisions to purchase equipment you want.

The challenge is that sometimes you need to purchase new equipment when you don't have money and sometimes you shouldn't purchase when you do have money.

For sound equipment and capital purchases you need to go back to your 10x rule business plan and look at your big picture. Have you identified the need for this equipment? Do you need a new server, car, custom application, or set of furniture, etc.?

What are your identified NEEDS, not wants, for the growth and sustainability of your bigger business? When do they come into the plan? Is it now, in the future, or is it not part of your plan at all?

Look at your growth numbers. How big will your business be when specific purchases are necessary?

You want to purchase a needed item just before it is necessary, not years before you need it.

Grow with intention and use your strategy to create your growth schedule.

The #2 Rule of Decision Making: **Use tools**
Two Tools: the SWOT and the Decision Matrix

There are many tools you can use to help evaluate a decision. I like tools that help me see the big picture. I'd like to describe a SWOT analysis in a way you would not usually consider using it, and a decision matrix I often use, recommend, and teach.

[A] SWOT Analysis and Other Tools

Let's say I decide I'll hire sometime in the future. There are many tools and assessments to help you define how well someone will fit into your business (like DISC[8]), how others perceive a candidate (like "How to Fascinate[9]"), and your candidate's cognitive style (like "Myers Briggs[10]"). Use the tools to find the best fit for your working style and business culture.

I also like to use a SWOT analysis for hiring decisions. SWOT (Strengths, Weaknesses, Opportunities, and Threats) analysis is traditionally used to evaluate your business or your competition. I like to use it to evaluate people and relationships. You can find a blank SWOT chart in the resources section at the end of this book. The SWOT analysis evaluates your relationship value (or the candidate's) to the company. Here's how I use it:

S = Strength

What are your strengths? List your hard and soft skills, your degrees, accreditations, and certifications. List your emotional and leadership strengths. For instance, I am: technically inclined, scientifically trained, possessed of high emotional intelligence, and I like and am liked by most people I meet.

---

[8] DISC Assessment (See DISC assessment online for personal testing sights)

[9] How to Fascinate (http://www.howtofascinate.com/)

[10] Myers Briggs (http://www.myersbriggs.org/my-mbti-personality-type/mbti-basics/)

W = Weaknesses

This is the place where you find it hard to function. Where could you use more training, where are you lacking in skill, ability, emotional strength, support, or leadership?

I have overcome a lot of the weaknesses I had around doubting my self-worth. Always feeling others were more worthy than me made it difficult to step into a new opportunity and impossible to grow my business. I am still working on other weaknesses I have around money.

O = Opportunity

What opportunities do you have for personal growth? Do you have a great mentor, an "in" at a university or college, an invitation to do something you have never done before? Where can you go to learn, or experience, personal growth?

While writing this chapter I was contacted by a successful business owner of whom I am very fond. She is focused and growing aggressively and she wanted me to do a joint venture with her for two years to create a product worth about $100,000 or more a year. It is so easy to say "no" right now as my time is pretty full, but I know that opportunities take time to evaluate so I'll put this opportunity on my pile for immediate investigation. This is one of the opportunities in my SWOT analysis.

T = Threats

Where are you a threat to your business? One of my clients works with a leader, let's call him Frank (not his real name), who tends to be very controlling. The threat to Frank's business lies in the way he aggressively attacks anyone who tries to make a decision. He often ends up agreeing with people, but the act of having to go through an argument just to do the work slows down the decision-making process for the entire company and will eventually lead to failure in services, delivery, and quality.

To resolve the situation with Frank, the company hired a strong, non-threatening woman to act as a buffer between Frank and the other employees. She fights his battles for him in a way that results in positive relationships with the employees, and she brings him to a place of agreement.

As a result, the company gets to move forward with ease. It is not ideal, but it is a reasonable solution and it helps neutralize the threat Frank poses to his employees and his company.

The SWOT tool is an excellent way to understand what you bring to your company. When it's time to make hiring decisions, find people who can work with your strengths, complement and support your weaknesses, help you evaluate your opportunities, and either offset or help eliminate your threats.

[B] Decision Matrix

In 1998, I found myself laid-off again. The high-tech industry was going through a shift and the dot-com tech-bubble was ready to burst. The internet was finally becoming a useful tool for all businesses, and change was becoming the "norm."

I had never expected to be employed by the same company for decades, but it was still a challenging time: I was just returning from a six-month maternity leave when I found out that my company was closing down. I went on employment benefits to help pay the bills while I looked for another opportunity.

Fortunately, I had a chance to spend some time with an employment counsellor who helped me determine the best fit for my needs, skills, and lifestyle. He introduced me to a tool called the decision matrix. I've used it, shared it, and taught it at college for many years to help people who are confused, torn, or overwhelmed by the decisions they are facing. It can be used for any type of decision that can affect your future.

The decision matrix is basically a way to evaluate your choices and their potential effect on your values. You get a score for each decision that will more clearly reflect how you feel about the option and how it may affect your life.

To use this tool, you need to know all of your options and all of the possible outcomes. I recommend you brainstorm ideas with a friend or colleague to ensure you get the full picture of what's available.

I'm going to demonstrate this tool using a personal decision matrix and a business decision matrix, both of which are fictional, yet which are based on decisions my clients have had to make in the past.

The important point to recognize is that the numbers only apply to you and no one else. It is your decision and your outcome.

Table 2 shows a decision matrix for a woman thinking about leaving her husband. If you are in a rocky business partnership, the options and outcomes might apply to you and your situation as well, since a partnership is very similar to a marriage.

Down the left side of the matrix are the issues that are important to this woman and that will be affected by her decision.

In this case we have listed the woman's values as her money, her children's well-being, her ability to have a house or home for herself and her kids, her personal time, her ability to travel, her health, her emotional balance, and her stress levels.

Across the top of the matrix is a list of her choices. When using this type of matrix, you must have more than two choices. When you do this for yourself, look for all of the outcomes that could apply to you so you get a broad understanding of your expectations and your needs.

For Table 2 there are several possible outcomes, including two that are extreme and unlikely — the woman will do nothing and the husband will leave town and never see his kids again. You need to look at all of the extreme options so you don't miss seeing a key decision factor that has been making your decision difficult.

Once all possible outcomes have been uncovered, we look at how each possible outcome affects each value. Put a "10" if it is a great option for that value and a "0" if it would have the worst possible outcome for that value.

In Table 2 you see that this woman would have lots of personal time if she were to "leave it all behind" and she would be emotionally compromised if she was to "continue as-is." She evaluates her children's well-being as only a "5" if the couple were to stay together and a "5" if they divorce. She does not see any option that makes her children happier, at least during the time of this decision. Money is at its best outcome if she does not move out, but her health and stress levels are critically low, likely indicating that there are a lot of arguments and negative emotional interactions taking place. If the woman chooses not to make any changes, she must then be willing to accept all of these challenges.

Now take a look at the "Divorce" column. Although the kids are no better off and money is a lot tighter for the family as it tries to manage two households, her personal time goes up (as she expects to share custody) and her health, happiness, emotional well-being, and stress levels are also better.

When the columns are totalled, the best option, based on this person's expectations, situation, relationships, and willingness to make changes, is to "Divorce" (an option that scored 55 points). The worst-case scenario for this person is to "Continue As-Is" (which generated a score of 33). When we understand how we are affected by the outcome of our choices we can make better decisions.

Table 2: Personal-Type Decision to Leave

	Continue AS-IS	Separate and move	Separate and stay	Divorce	Leave it all behind
Kids	5	3	4	5	0
Money	7	3	7	3	1
Home/House	7	6	7	6	5
Personal Time	3	7	5	7	10
Travel	6	2	6	2	8
Health	4	6	4	8	6
Emotional	0	8	3	8	3
Stress	1	6	3	8	6
Totals	33	49	42	55	45

Now look at Table 3. This is a decision matrix for deciding where to set up a small business office. This person has space at home for an office that includes a door to close off intrusions. This person also has access to renting an office, sharing office space, or taking part-time membership in a business centre.

The business centre offers a desk to work at, but it is shared with other people so personal effects cannot be left onsite. It is a transient office with phones, meeting rooms, and other technology available for a price. The other three alternatives are permanent office spaces.

If you look at the final tally for the options, notice that the business centre initially is a clear winner (Sub-Total 67), yet the office space chosen was to "Work from Home" because the cost factor was more heavily weighted for a new business. Again, being close to family and available for kids weighted very high for the "Work from Home" option.

Since this person stopped commuting in order to be closer to their kids, it also was more heavily weighted.

The important thing to know is that when you calculate your #1 option it may more clearly represent a future option rather than the next one. Knowing the future goal based on a decision matrix will help when you go to level-up.

What was not taken into account when the matrix was done was Security, Privacy and Convenience. This person did not know how important these values would be to their business until after they had been in business for a while. Once that was calculated, the "Work from Home" option was a clear choice (Total 84).

Table 3 Business-Type Decision - Where to Locate

	Work from Home	Lease Space	Share Space	Business Centre
Cost	10	1	4	4
Clients	0	9	9	9
Professional Image	1	9	9	9
Motivation	6	7	9	9
Energy	6	6	6	7
Family	10	6	6	6
Health	7	2	2	7
Income	7	2	4	7
Happiness	10	0	4	9
Subtotal	57	42	53	67
Security	7	7	5	0
Privacy	10	10	8	5
Convenience	10	7	6	2
Total	84	66	72	74

I use this tool to evaluate key capital purchases, hire new contractors, buy new computers or a car, or make significant changes to my business focus, new time commitments, volunteering, joint ventures, and so much more. Try it for your next decision!

The # 3 Rule of Decision Making: Expert Insight

I often find that new business owners ask people they trust for advice on making decisions, but these individuals have neither the desire to run a business nor the skill or experience to do so. Their advice is filtered through the lens of a secure job and a regular income. Investment is a gamble that most people only do well when purchasing mutual funds, and that is because there is an expert making choices for them. Business owners have more control over their business success than investors have over the value of their retirement savings! Giving away your power as a business owner by allowing your friends and loved ones to have powerful input into decisions relating to your business can be the start of failure.

I spoke with a business owner once who had been in business for 17 years. She was ready for a huge change in her business and she knew she needed to do things differently. **She was overwhelmed and overworked**. She wanted to work with me, in fact she even said, "You are what I need right now." But when it came time to step up, she could not make the decision. Her husband offered to work for her over the summer, when he was off from his teaching job and instead of getting strategic advice, she took him on in her business. The challenge here is that she was looking for expert experience and insight, and she took operational help instead because it was what her *husband* thought she needed, knowing how overworked she was. His love for her made him want to help in the only way he knew how, but her need to increase her business was not tied to doing the work, it was tied to creating new streams of income. Be confident that you can make good decisions. This will give you a better ability to do what is best for your business growth.

Barb, your book Entrepreneur Awakening is right on the money. The techniques and tools you offer give direction that most entrepreneurs ask me about on a consistent basis. It's about focus, targeting what's important in the now, and building for a brilliant future. I liken the decision to veer from employee to entrepreneur to moving from the passenger seat, simply along for the ride, to taking control of the wheel and making decisions on where you're going, and what you'll see. It's about chasing your passion instead of simply earning a pay cheque. In my 27 years of policing I discovered that, though I had loved the work, I hated the internal politics. As a result, I never wrapped my identity up in my occupation. It didn't define me. Yes, I worked as a cop, but I was so much more. I was a free thinking (definitely way outside the box), highly motivated, dad, husband, son, uncle, coach, writer, artist and musician. My kids call me artsy-Farrah. That's me. That's my passion. Policing paid the bills. It was me on a treadmill and I was dying a death of a thousand paper cuts. My passion was in helping others achieve stability, safety and growth, ridding the world of the term "victim", yes, all extensions of policing if I wanted to extend my reach in that manner. I learned the value of being proactive instead of reactive. That's what the crux of your book is about – chasing that passion. It's seeing what's down the road and preparing yourself for the goals you want to achieve. Being proactive instead of reactive. You can earn a paycheque, or you can live a life of passion."

- **Brian Trainor** retired Police Sergeant - Cyberbully Prevention lecturer / Elder Fraud Prevention expert

Chapter 10: When to Level-up

> *The ladder to success isn't a ladder, it is a succession of steps with leaps in between.*
> **- Seth Godin**

When we start a new business, we are focused on making it work. We have an idea of the level of success we wish to accomplish. People often base the success of their new small business on their perceived value as an employee in their most successful position. I've heard people say, "I just want to make $50,000 per year," or "I'm so busy, I can't take any more clients." The challenge with limited expectations is that it is hard to grow easily when growth is needed.

The best time to plan to level-up is right now. Start with a plan for growth so you can manage the clients that come to you. If you start turning customers away they will find an alternative to you, and getting them back will take more effort and dollars than expected. The result is that you will stay on your income rollercoaster much longer.

There is a balance between always growing and never having enough to grow. This makes many of us afraid of success. After all, what if we get what we want? What do we have to give up, or lose, to maintain that new success? That kind of unknown change is enough to stop us from doing the work or even looking at the plan to do the work.

Always and Never

A lot of people expect that when they get their new business up and running it will grow, but the reality is it will grow to a preconceived level and stick there. We've worked hard to keep the business at that level and it's stressful to push it farther.

This is a common challenge. Growth is not a one-time dream – it is a full-time commitment. To be fully engaged and committed to business growth you must have a plan to be in fulltime launch: launching new events, products, services, sales, ad campaigns, etc. This means you must implement your growth strategy again and again.

What does a growth strategy look like? A growth strategy requires insight into what your business will look like at the 10x model. If you don't remember your numbers, or what your 10x strategy model looks like, go back to the chapter "Chapter 8: Think Big." Levelling-up means implementing the next phase of your business. This is often incredibly hard as the next phase of your growth usually requires resources that you believe you cannot afford until you are at that next level. It is a "Catch-22" for many, and it's often the reason why growth stalls for most businesses.

How do we create a step where a leap is required? I have an amazing client who manufactures an incredible and unique granola with her husband. Fran Kruse runs *Not Yer Granny's Granola & Snack Co.* and she has successfully created a local market with committed clients. She also has a dream of owning a food manufacturing and distribution company but she became stalled at the local distribution stage. Her home province of Ontario has labelling laws that require food manufacturers to list nutritional facts and other information in both French and English. If she were to distribute her granola outside her region, she'd have to change her labelling.

Fran already had thousands of her original bags and labels and she was renting a commercial kitchen in the evenings because she did not have her own. She knew her current process of manually applying labels and cooking every night wouldn't be realistic if she wanted to sell in a larger market like Toronto. Her plan was to wait six months and try and sell more product locally so she could then get a new brand for her new printed bags and a kitchen of her own.

That certainly qualified as a level-up plan, but it's one I don't always recommend. People often wait in the hope of creating more income using the same strategies they have in place. A growth plan with no leap usually generates little or no growth. If you are waiting and hoping to have enough money to do something big in your business then you likely cannot see all the details of your 10x strategy plan in your level-up plan.

When we looked at Fran's numbers, it was clear she was trying to take three big steps all at the same time. Producing new labeling takes three months, completing the branding for new bags takes a few months as well, and a new kitchen comes with a large price tag. To try and attempt this all at once meant Fran needed an investor. But without significant presales and contracts, it was going to be hard to attract one.

When we broke Fran's goals down into smaller chunks, each step became easier and less costly, and the project became much more manageable.

The key was to find the linchpin in the plan, the one thing that had to get done to make forward motion possible. Fran absolutely could not sell in Toronto without new labelling, but she could increase her sales in Toronto without new branding or a new kitchen.

With this information, the labelling became the biggest priority. The estimated cost of translating the labels and printing them on new bags was about $5,000. This was money she could raise immediately. If she didn't have to stick labels on bags, she would have more time to find new clients in Toronto. So, her new strategy became:

1. Get labels translated

2. Get new bags printed

3. Reach out to 10 vendors per week to arrange a sample drop-off with decision-makers.

4. Drop off samples and invite the vendors to sign up for a three- or six-month trial purchase at a reduced price. The goal would be to pre-sell at least 100 bags per month in the Toronto area, starting in two months.

The labeling and printing took a couple of months to complete, during which time Fran was able to get out and pre-sell orders for the Toronto market. This shaved at least six months off her wait for new market sales. Her project is not yet complete but she recently gave me an update on how things have been going. I've paraphrased her a little, but here's what's happened since we worked together on her plan a year ago.

A Follow Up on Fran's Granola

Being an entrepreneur means being flexible and fluid....stuff 'happens' and 'quickly'.
Fran Kruse

It took Fran three months to organize the translations, graphics, labels, packaging, manufacturing and printing. In that time, she did try to reach out to Toronto vendors but found she had limited success dealing directly with the stores.

Undaunted, she found a distributor who already had connections with vendors in Toronto. This person loved the product and was easily able to get the granola into their own customers' stores.

Now Fran's granola is sold in stores from North Bay to Niagara Falls, plus the company is still contacting some retailers directly on its own. As for the kitchen, Fran and her husband had spent almost two years baking at night and on weekends, and they knew this was no way to service all their new sales. Plus, they were exhausted. Fran was excited to tell me they had just received the keys to their own kitchen space.

"Now I might even get a weekend off," she says.

Talk about dedication!

"Having our own kitchen will allow us to expand our product line to include other snacks like cookies, crackers, nuts and chocolate...which opens up other markets."

Congratulations Fran, you and your husband are amazing entrepreneurs!

If you are waiting for money to enter your business through increased sales, then it is likely you will never be able to level-up. Add your new market with the resources you have now and use those sales (or pre-sales) to create value in your business so you can either afford to level-up again or be in a better place to ask for investment.

Having a unique and valuable product or service will not attract investors' money. Having a plan for growth and guaranteed sales will.

Transition Point

What does a transition point look like? How do I plan for it? Transition points are the place in your business where you realize you can't...

- do any more business

- handle any more clients

- manufacture any more product

- deliver any more services

... because you need more resources. These are the resources you cannot afford at the current level. It is the transition point because you need to do more to grow your business, yet you can't afford the associated costs. This is the most misunderstood key to growth and it's an endless circle: you need to work to pay for a bigger business that can transact more sales — which you cannot manage without more investment — which you cannot afford without more sales. This is a dangerous, slippery mindset.

Growth happens in these three steps:

1. Invest

↓

2. Implement

↓

3. Grow

That means that your transition point happens at the investment stage. You must accept that the investment, whether it shows up as more money or more time, or both, is your first step.

I find that most business owners are stuck at a specific level because they do not have more time or more money. In the words of The Oracle from the movie *The Matrix*, "Bingo. It is a pickle. No doubt about it."

There are thousands of ways to find resources in your business and if you start with a mindset of "how can I...?" instead of "I wish I could...," then opportunities will start finding you.

Finding Resources

1. Look for ways of breaking your transitional goal into smaller tasks. Fran started with a smaller investment that led to more resources she could use for the next step. This meant getting her product to a new market at least six months earlier than planned, and it allowed her to generate funds for her next steps, re-branding and getting a new kitchen.

2. Hire for non-skilled work first. If you are doing work in your business that requires minimal training and therefore could be hired out at a lower rate, then you can free up some of your time to put into your transition.

3. Automate and create systems. This will also free up time for you and the people working for you. If you do anything manually that can be handled by a free or inexpensive app or software, then look into making that happen first.

4. Look at what else you can sell, or other potential customers. This might include:

   - A different package size

   - A different market location

   - A different distribution site

   - Electronic online delivery of a service instead of in-person

     a. Can you give someone a commission to sell your products? If your products are online, then offer an affiliate commission and get your products into new hands. If someone else is doing the sales, or some of these sales, then you have more time.

The key to these strategies is that they either create more income or save you time that you can put towards your transition.

Taking a smaller step will cost you significantly less than going right for your next big step, freeing up capital and time for your big growth steps.

Don't put off growth for later or it will likely never happen. You must always be in growth mode, working through your transition points.

In the words of Darren Hardy, "If you aren't improving you're falling behind."

Wrap-up (Part II)

During the implementation stage, you will begin by wearing most of the hats in your business, and this will start you on the road to your transformation.

You will become the person who can instigate change, not only in your business but in your home, in your community, and maybe even in the world.

The mindset you are starting to embrace will likely allow you to experience less fear of change overall, and fewer hurt feelings when a family member suggests to you "get a real job."

If you have not done it yet, go back to the chapter "Take Action" and complete your desire statement, define your goals for the business and write out your accomplishments.

If you skip doing the work now it will indicate that you are willing to skip doing work that does not seem important.

The most successful entrepreneurs don't skip work that they cannot evaluate. Do this new work to understand its value to you so you are better able to make the big decisions later.

Part III - Live It

> As the CEO, you cannot simply do YOUR work in your
> business, you must ensure ALL the work gets done.
> - **Barb Stuhlemmer**

So now you are a business owner. You have created something that is unique, with a plan to make it grow and be profitable. What else is there? Well, lifestyle of course.

We are very familiar with the lifestyle we had before we started a business. We also know what we want. We dream of a business that runs like clock-work, ticking through the motions of creation, sales, and delivery. We see the lifestyle we can have when we get to do something we love and make money at it. And how about spending that money? Oh yes, we have a vision for that too. But what quickly happens for many entrepreneurs is that we lose boundaries and balance.

Many struggle with the question of when to say "no," when to shut things down, and when to stop or move on. That's OK, because either the business owner learns all of the above and gains some control, or he or she lives it all without the control. In Part III of this book —"Live It"— I want to help you better understand what you are taking on. It is not a job, it is a lifestyle.

Like losing weight, playing an instrument, or starting a new hobby, you have to learn all there is to know about your business, practice your new rituals daily, and learn to fail and then try again.

There is no truly right way to do this, as everyone's business goals and life goals are different. But there are some things you can do to make it easier to get it right for you.

"Everything you do in your business should help lead to more sales. Every hat you and other people in your business wear should lead to more sales. Don't leave any hat unworn. Don't leave any work undone. Running a business is not about being an employee, it is about creating a place where employees are needed. "

- Barb Stuhlemmer

Chapter 11: Whose Hat is it?

The first rule of estimating the intelligence of a ruler is to look at the men he has around him.
 - **Niccolò Machiavelli, The Prince**

Once you have all the fundamentals in place, the routine of running your business will begin. If you expect to be successful, this will take a lot of your time.

Startups have many moving parts and you are the conductor of them all.

As a small business owner, you will be required to wear many hats in your business, and you cannot ignore one just because you are not good at it or you don't like it.

A business only runs well when all areas of the company run well.

I was on an intake call recently with a woman who was very well-read and had a PhD.

She had written four books and she was passionate about who she served and what she had to offer. She knew she needed to reach more people, yet she balked at the idea of creating a marketing plan.

"I already do networking, I just have to make more connections and build better relationships," she told me.

Her four books were not yet best sellers and she felt she just needed to put them on Amazon to make that happen.

She was the "Doer" of the marketing work but not the conductor of her marketing team. As a sole-proprietor with no employees, she had not accepted the marketing management hat as one she MUST wear.

I could hear her fear as I kept pointing out this missing link. "You cannot just show up and expect clients to find you, you must have a plan to meet them, engage them, and invite them to take an action," I told her.

She finally agreed, but I think it was just to get me to stop talking so she could quietly put the project off into the future again. And that is what she did. To this day she does no marketing and she is not a best-seller.

Let's look a little closer at this idea of "wearing many hats." Here is a list of typical positions in your business—some of the hats you might wear:

- CEO, CFO, COO
- Accountant/Bookkeeper/Clerk
- Receptionist/Admin
- Project manager
- Product or service development manager
- Product or service manufacturing manager
- Product or service delivery manager
- Customer sales/support/service manager
- Accounts receivable and payable manager
- Inventory/supplies manager
- Contracts/Legal manager
- Manager of human resources/contractors

If you truly hate a position, and doing the work would be detrimental to your company, then hire it out. It must get done and it will get done better, faster, and with fewer errors by someone who loves the work.

Like the woman on my intake call, you cannot simply create the programs, offer the courses, or write the books... you have to market them, sell them, deliver them, etc.

People need to know what you have to offer, and how they can make a purchase.

You cannot simply create an event and leave it at that; you must invite people to attend and then follow up afterwards.

You cannot simply provide incredible service, like long-term therapy, house painting, coaching, training or consulting, etc.

You must also allocate your time between you, your clients, your marketing, your prospects, your employees and contractors, your referral partners, and all the people with whom you have relationships in your business.

Everything you do in your business should help lead to more sales. Every hat you and other people in your business wear should lead to more sales. Don't leave any hat unworn. Don't leave any work undone.

Running a business is not about being an employee, it is about creating a place where employees are needed.

Put on your CEO hat first, create the skeleton of your business by identifying the positions that must be filled, and then assign a person to each position, even if that person is you at first.

Accept the roles and do the work.

If you have to learn something new, then learn it, but do not ignore a role, or else you are removing a key piece from your business machine and, ultimately, from your sales.

"If you thought you were going to lose your house, your clients, and your wife and kids, you would stop doing the work too. The thoughts are not rational, but they are very common and they happen in varying degrees to all people at all levels of business. The key is to keep the irrational thoughts from preventing you from taking action. Knowing you may miss a mortgage payment should be more than enough motivation to make sure you do the work to make the money. "

- Barb Stuhlemmer

Chapter 12 Embrace the Fear

Definition modified from Google:
"Fear is an unpleasant emotion caused by the belief that someone or something is dangerous, likely to cause pain, or is a threat to one's self, one's attachments (including things and loved ones), or one's way of life."

Fear is an action-killer. It is the instigator of procrastination and an emotion that can cause us to do things we would never rationally do. Fear can be the seed of stress that germinates into a breakdown or illness. Fear can stop us from doing what has to get done, from acting on opportunity, and from mending a relationship. To fear something is to worry about something that has not happened—or may never happen—so deeply that you miss making the right things happen.

Daniel Kahneman, the author of *Thinking Fast and Slow* talks about the research that defines how our brains can make fast decisions and how we can slow down our thinking to get more details and information. When it comes to fear, the slow-thinking part of our brain is in overload, trying to understand and work out how we can avoid the pain we expect to happen and are not yet experiencing. In this example from Seth Godin's book *The Icarus Deception* he tells a story of his summers at camp as a youth. He explains how campers would climb a 22-foot-high ladder to a diving board but then be completely paralyzed when it came time to jump. Once a camper made their first jump, however, the next jump was easier. The slow brain did not have to spend any more time deciding on all the ways it could die. The path was known, the outcome was safe and fun, and the decision-making was now faster and easier.

Fear is a big factor in decision-making for new business owners as the experience and the outcomes are still foreign and unknown. The fast brain cannot make the decision because there is not enough experience to see the outcome clearly, so the brain hands it over to the slow brain for evaluation. The slow brain, which includes the lizard brain (also described by Seth Godin in an earlier book, *Lynchpin*), starts looking at all the possibilities. The thought process may look like this:

What you see as needed and why	What you evaluate as a possible outcome when there is fear.	What your lizard brain says.
I need to invest money to start or grow my business.	If I invest too much money and I don't make enough I might miss my mortgage payment.	I could lose my house and my kids will be without a place to live.
I have to make sales calls to get more clients and bring in more money.	I might offend people by getting them at the wrong time.	They will never purchase from me when they see I am a pushy, interrupting sales person.
I have to put long hours into the beginning of this project to get it complete and make money quickly.	I should be able to do this in less time. If I put in too much time people will see me as incompetent and slow.	This will be my life for as long as I have this business. My wife will leave me and my kids will not understand why I am never available. I'm a bad parent and husband.

If you thought you were going to lose your house, your clients, and your wife and kids, you would stop doing the work too. The thoughts are not rational, but they are very common and they happen in varying degrees to all people at all levels of business.

The key is to keep the irrational thoughts from preventing you from taking action. Knowing you may miss a mortgage payment should be more than enough motivation to make sure you do the work to make the money.

- Losing your house because of bad strategies takes a lot of poor decisions and missed opportunities. Having the key team members and mentors in place will help reduce these risks.

- Losing clients because you are a pushy salesperson on the phone means you need to invest in a great sales coach. Someone from whom others love to buy.

- Losing your wife and kids because you never have time means you have not implemented a plan. If you have one, then you need to bring them in on the plan so they can see the timelines and the outcomes, as well as the deadlines for your return to their lives.

If you cannot make any of this happen, then you are allowing your fear to direct your actions. Fear is a lonely emotion. Get out and talk to people about what you are experiencing. Knowing you are not alone will start changing your idea of what you can do to make things better and open up new opportunities.

Running Out of Money

Whether you are an investor-supported business or you are self-invested there is always a concern about money.

- What has to be purchased?

- What expenses are required?

- What sales are expected?

- What revenue is needed?

- Is there a cash flow?

The last of these questions is the most valuable, and knowing the answer will help you focus on the investment, expenses, and effort require to win your clients and succeed in your business growth.

In my first company (ClearComm Information Design) I initially had a really hard time getting new clients, which made it hard to justify some of the investments I wanted to make. After all, if there was no money coming in, then the money going out was my personal money. To top it off, that money was part of my husband's earnings and sometimes earmarked for family events and purchases. Taking money from the family coffers to put into my business was a difficult decision to make when guilt played a big part of the process. It can get even more difficult as the money becomes tighter and debt is a reality.

Six years into ClearComm I had an opportunity to transition into business development for small business owners and I took it. Starting BLITZ Business Success was the right fit for me. I had $10,000 ear-marked for ClearComm marketing when I made my transition to business development and support services. I decided to use that money to start BLITZ instead. Fast-forward three years and I found myself at the hardest time I have ever had to face in my life financially. I felt hurt and frustrated by my inability to create consistent cash flow, and painfully guilty to have accumulated a large amount of debt, both in BLITZ and in my personal life as well. How could I run out of money? I had a big plan, people loved me, and I was creating huge change. I love what I do and I am great at it, too.

Money is not the be-all and end-all but without money the wheels of progress are slow and they sometimes stop.

- I can't afford to travel (but I need to).

- I can't afford to run events (but my clients expect them)

- I can't afford a membership (but I have to belong because my clients do)

- I can't afford event registration (but I cannot afford to miss the event. For my business, not being seen is the same as not being in business.)

If you know you have a bigger calling to fulfil in life, then it is your duty to not run out of money. It would be a disservice to all of those you could be helping, so you must find a way to continue to generate income and make your business bring value. Getting on track takes a lot of discipline and intention. I have a three-step process that will help you stay on track, or get back on track, if you are already feeling the sting of debt.

1. STOP

2. EVALUATE

3. PLAN

STOP

I started by putting on the spending brakes. No credit card use, except for business purchases that required it (e.g. my online shopping cart software). "The Brakes" means a hard stop on buying whatever seems needed, which means spending consciously.

I knew that I was committed to paying a lot of expenses because of contracts or operational expenses (e.g. I had leases, insurance, and gas for my car). I also knew that I had invested deeply into some big development changes that had not showed a quick return. I could not continue that type of investment until I developed better plans that ensured a return on investment. If you pay for nothing you get nothing, so keep paying for your needed expenses but stop making additional investments that don't have a good ROI.

Conscious spending takes effort and an awareness of your required expenses. If you need help understanding where to spend and where to stop spending, read the Evaluation section which follows.

I stopped doing anything new and focused on maximizing the opportunities inherent in the investments I had already paid for.

- My Chamber of Commerce membership was paid up until the end of the year – I decided to network there, rather than invest in additional networking.

- I had speaking engagements booked at associations – I decided to pay to be at earlier events before I spoke in order to help raise my brand image to the members and increase interest in my talk.

Basically, I focused on anything that was already paid for and was also potentially a revenue-generating event. The biggest "Aha" I had was that although my time is valuable and limited, it is free to me. Getting on the phone and calling the people on my list, past clients, and new connections was my number one task. It was a good start, and yet I was still bleeding money, behind in some payments, painfully stretched, and emotionally overwhelmed. This was not enough, so after STOP I started the EVALUATION.

EVALUATE

If you want to create conscious spending you have to be aware of what must be spent. Understanding your numbers is key when debt and financial overwhelm is upon you.

Start by gathering all of your business and personal numbers.

Business Expenses

- Loans & leases

- Membership payments (e.g. Chamber of Commerce)

- Regular meeting costs (monthly Chamber breakfast)

- Online tools (Skype credit, shopping cart, website)

- Necessities (phone, cell, office space, gas)

- Carrying costs (inventory, contract commitments)

- Professional services (accounting, legal)

- Staff (contractors, employees, outsourcing)

- Your wage (Yes, pay yourself!)

- Taxes[11]

Add up all your expenses and determine what the summary cost is as a monthly payment.

Here are three examples:

My Chamber membership is a yearly expense. I take the cost of that payment and I divide it by 12 to get the monthly amount.

$$\$360 \div 12 \text{ months} = \$30/\text{month}$$

The Chamber's events occur twice per month. I take their associated costs and multiply by two to get the monthly amount.

$$\$20 \times 2 \text{ per month} = \$40/\text{month}$$

If you have a weekly payment commitment (for example $24/week), then multiply by the number of weeks in the year you pay and divide by 12 months to get the monthly payment.

$$\$24 \text{ per week for 52 weeks}$$

$$\$24 \times 52 \div 12 = \$104/\text{month}$$

Now add up all the monthly payments:

$$\$30 + \$20 + \$104 = \$154$$

This is the number you use to get ahead of your payments. In this example, you need to be putting away $154/month to cover your costs for the year.

---

[11] Sales taxes are not included here. When tax is collected on a sale it should be immediately put aside for payment to the government. That money is never yours.

By the end of the year there will be enough in your account to cover your Chamber membership and to have covered all other payments throughout the year.

Business Income

- List all products/services you can sell

- List the price of each

- What is the actual selling frequency of each?

Calculate the amount of money you expect to have coming in monthly. It needs to be bigger than the monthly expenses or you will be losing money.

In the above example, the income will need to be bigger than $154/month to cover the expenses and to make a profit.

Business Assets and Liabilities
Does your company own any assets, like a vehicle, property, computer systems, inventory, etc.? It is important to understand where your money is in your company in case there is a need for money someday.

List all your debts: credit cards with a balance, line of credit, contracts with required payments, loans, mortgages, etc.

No one ever wants to have to liquidate their assets to pay off bad debt, but knowing where the value is and what you owe can help in challenging times and can often help you completely avoid challenging times.\

Personal
Look at your personal numbers as well. You will want to understand all the costs and income available to you as a person because what I have found in small business is that we personally support the growth of our startup with our own money until it is stable and profitable. Unfortunately, many small businesses never reach this point and often it is because their owners don't understand all the numbers, including their own financial limitations.

Personal Expenses

Use the example in the evaluation of the business section above to figure out how much you are spending every month. Look at all payments:

- Utilities (phone, electricity, water, gas)

- Taxes

- Mortgage

- Insurance

- Children's expenses (clothes, school, sports)

- Food

- Vehicle maintenance and fuel

- Tithings

You can add everything up and determine how much you need to put away monthly to cover your own personal costs.

In some households, paycheques come in every two weeks, not monthly, and some people know their expenses as a bi-weekly number. It is a little more complicated to figure out this number, but it lets you know what you have to put away every two weeks to cover your expenses. I like this idea, because when the paycheque comes in, the expenses are deducted immediately. It never gets into your spending stream. This way payments are not missed.

For example, if your property taxes are billed four times a year at $975, you should determine the yearly amount (multiply by 4), divide by 52 weeks, and multiply by two to get the amount you need to put away every two weeks. You then know that you have to put away $150 every two weeks just to cover your quarterly tax payments.

Personal Income

Look at all income streams in your household. Again, your personal income should cover your personal expenses.

Assets and Liabilities

List your personal assets (like the equity in your home, other properties, vehicles etc.) and your current liabilities (like your mortgage, car loan, etc.)

Your personal net worth is your assets minus your liabilities. Your banker should be able to help you define this number, or you may be able to find tools on your bank's website to help you do this calculation yourself.

PLAN

Running out of money is caused by two issues:

1. The lack of money to continue.

2. The lack of a plan to ensure there is never a lack of money

You might think, "well, if I continue to invest while I'm building my business and customer base, how can a plan ensure I don't run out of money?" It can't! But what it can do is show you when you are going to run out of money and give you the insight into what has to happen, by when, to ensure you are on the right path — or possibly when to leave the path.

It may be that you don't get the sales you expect after trying a product launch. How long will you continue to sell something that does not seem to appeal to the market you are targeting? How much effort should you put into more marketing, finding different strategies to reach your clients, or finding a new target market?

At what point do you say to yourself, "that's enough"?

You have likely heard the concept of "Fail early and fail often." I know John C. Maxwell has talked about this, and other mentors have as well.

Not many people like the thought of failure, so instead of recognizing they have failed, a business owner will often continue until they cannot go on any longer. They will carry on instead of changing their business model, so they don't appear to be distracted or incompetent.

In software manufacturing, there is a system called a "fail-fast." Jim Shore[12], a columnist for IEEE Software explains this system as "a system that is designed to immediately report at its interface any failure or condition that is likely to lead to a failure." The fail-fast must be programed to recognize what a failure looks like. In your business, ask yourself what a failure looks like. Is it one month without sales, six months running in the negative, two years without a profit, five years without pay? What is it? What are your "fail-fast" system's metrics?"

And if your fail-fast does get triggered, what will you do? Really, you only have two choices:

1. Continue on and eventually run out of money.

2. Make a significant change, including the possibility of closing your business, before you run out of money.

To be able to make an intelligent decision here you must know what your plan is, when you will make changes, what success looks like, and what your fail-fast trigger is.

Plan for failure, by knowing what it is, and work to avoid it so you don't run out of money before you become successful.

---

[12] http://www.martinfowler.com/ieeeSoftware/failFast.pdf

"It is not enough to talk about your dream, carry goal cards, or repeat affirmations. It is not enough to simply take action. Things only get done when you show up to complete the work. Self-awareness is the start of a life of reflection-understanding. If you believe you can do something, you will, if you don't believe you can, you won't. Showing up is the result of believing you can. Showing up is how you get to take action on your plan and be aware of your desire, day in and day out. It is how you appear to others and manifest a successful business and life. "
- **Barb Stuhlemmer**

Chapter 13 Show Up

> *If you want people to know who you are, you need to show up as someone first.*
> *- **Barb Stuhlemmer***

To show up means to be present for:

- Prospects
- JV partners
- Affiliates
- Customers/clients

- Employees
- Suppliers
- Family / friends
- Yourself

in all of these ways:

- Desire
- Action
- Planning

- Self-awareness
- Emotions
- Commitment

Showing up is the way to keep moving forward towards your goal.

It is not enough to desire to create something. Desire supports momentum but it cannot create it.

It is not enough to sit and plan and draw and design.

Ruth and Sheldon

I have a story I want to tell you about my dear friends Ruth and Sheldon. My husband and I lived next to Ruth and Sheldon for many years before we had children. They were lovely neighbours and friends. We didn't do a lot of things together as we were significantly younger than they were, but we loved spending an evening here and there chatting about what was going on in our lives. When we had our first child, Ruth would come and watch Connor if I had to run an errand. Not long after, our second child, Jack, was born and we decided to move to a larger home.

Sheldon ran his own business for several decades. It was a rag reclamation and cleaning supply store and it was quite successful. He had five employees and yet he spent long days and some weekends at the store. Ruth looked after the home. She had raised their two sons, who were now both grown and married. She kept an immaculate home and beautiful gardens, and she was always perfectly dressed and manicured. Her main job was to look after Sheldon. After all, she had been married to him since she was 17, almost 50 years. He was her life and she was his.

When Sheldon was close to 70 years old, just before we moved away, Ruth came home from a doctor's appointment with news that she had cancer and could expect to live for only six months more. Within three months, she was gone. It was devastating for Sheldon, as he kept recalling that their plans for retirement involved selling the business, buying an RV, and travelling across Canada. He not only had no partner with whom to fulfill his plans for retirement, but also the person who had looked after him was gone. He had to learn how to cook for himself, use appliances, and manage the home and gardens. He was lost without her.

Two years after she passed, Sheldon came to our home, as he often did. It was a warm summer's day and Sheldon drove up in a silver le Baron convertible with a blue interior. It was a beautiful car and Sheldon was happier than I had seen him in a long time.

> *I asked Sheldon, "What's with the new car?" Sheldon said he was never going to allow his work to interfere with what was important in life. He had given up his retirement with Ruth because he had not sold his business, and he was not going to miss out again. From that moment forward Sheldon planned for his succession in the business. He sold it and, after a two-year transition period, he moved to Jerusalem to be with his son. He was finally free of his business. He was happy and living his life.*

Ruth and Sheldon's plan of crossing the country in their RV and living their retirement out in the beauty of Canada was not enough to make it happen.

It is not enough to talk about your dream, carry goal cards, or repeat affirmations. It is not enough to simply take action.

Things only get done when you show up to complete the work.

Self-awareness is the start of a life of reflection-understanding. If you believe you can do something, you will, if you don't believe you can, you won't. Showing up is the result of believing you can. Showing up is how you get to take action on your plan and be aware of your desire, day in and day out. It is how you appear to others and manifest a successful business and life.

How to Show Up for Others

When I started my business, I felt like I was implementing a lot of new ideas, systems, processes, strategies, etc. It was great. I would get one after another implemented and I could stroke each one off my list.

- Create a product – check.
- Strategize a marketing campaign – check.
- Implement a new brand strategy – check.

My checklist was getting shorter and all that would be left to do when all items were completed was to sign up new clients and provide my service or product. One of my hardest challenges lay around how difficult I found the repetitive and redundant act of showing up. Every aspect of business is implemented, revisited, reworked and reapplied over and over.

Like the sales process itself, there is no respite. I kept stopping after I did the work. I kept thinking to myself, "finally I got through this live event/dinner/ conference, etc. Now I can focus on something else." Except usually the "something else" included getting ready for the next live event, dinner or conference. I was working as a one-focus owner. The challenge with one focus is that there are many things that must be done all the time in business. You need a multiple-focus plan if you don't want other things to slip.

Show up in your sales, even when you are in the middle of a big contract. Show up in your marketing strategy and planning, even when you are in the middle of another marketing campaign. Show up in your process development, even when you are in the middle of a negotiation. If you leave any part of your business behind, your business cannot grow. There will be no new clients when you finish the contract, nothing new to attract new clients when your current campaign is over, no ongoing support or ways to offload work when you land that new, big client and you have to hire contractors to do the work. Show up when it is time to sell and when you are working on client retention. Show up to all the people in your company, and all those external to your business.

To Sell

It takes your brand between seven and 20 touchpoints to build awareness of your business offering with someone. Remember in the chapter on "The Basics," under item #10 "The Plan," we described touchpoints as "any aspect of your business that can be experienced by anyone that interacts with your business, including your customer."

If you want to continue to fill your sales funnel and have clients in your future, it is important that you show up in your marketing and in your sales process. My friend, coach, and closest mentor, Laura Gisborne, is fond of saying, "it is not sexy, once you have done it—it becomes a process of 'Rinse and Repeat.'" It is a consistent, day-after-day, week-after-week, month-after-month, and year-after-year process that never stops until you decide you don't want the business any longer. To be successful, you must show up consistently so you can ensure consistent sales.

Think of Coca-Cola or Hellmann's Mayonnaise. Both companies have been around more than 100 years, yet they continue to entertain us with commercials. They freshen their brand, change their offering, add new products, and create interest with contests and coupons. They show up, and keep showing up, because they expect to be in business for years to come.

To Retain

Have you ever bought something expensive, like a car, and then never seen or heard from the sales person again? Where did you go the next time you went to buy that product again? Two years ago, I bought a new Subaru. It was not an easy purchase as there were a lot of communication issues: the delivery date was wrong and the terms were confusing and misrepresented in our talks, for example. Once I had my car, I was in love. Two years have passed and I have never heard from my sales person. If he had ever called I would have said, "Yes Mike, I love my car, thanks for asking." This week I received an offer to trade my car in for a brand new car from someone else at the same dealership. I had never met this person, but he showed up. He invited me to learn more. He caught my attention, and because I did not feel any affinity for the first sales person, I did not hesitate to call the new person. What if they had been from a different dealership? What if they had been from a different car company? Not only did that lack of "showing up" lose Mike another sale, it could have lost the dealership another sale.

Check in: Are you and your people showing up for clients in all aspects of the relationship, before, during, and after the sale?

Internal

Have you ever worked in a large corporation? One of those businesses where you may not even know the names of all the people that work in your company? I have. I worked for a small company that was a division of a giant corporation. Our small piece of the corporation included about 50 people who maintained a core of trust and camaraderie. We all knew each other and we were a team.

But when a decision that affected all of us came down from the top of the faceless, nameless corporate ladder, there was unrest and gossip. People were unsure of the direction the company was taking, and they worried about their future. Finally, our internal manager, Harold, owned the decision himself. I have learned a lot about leadership from Harold. Harold constantly showed up. He was there for social events, even though his status clearly was not the same as all the people that worked for him. He kept showing up. He was available for discussions with staff, even though his role in the company required him to focus on bigger matters. And he engaged and listened as someone who really cared about each of us. He showed up. He shared details about the changing corporate direction, even though we really didn't need to be "in the know" — and that gave us a feeling of being valuable to the company. Harold modeled what it meant to show up. When Harold asked something of us, we all showed up, too.

If you're the boss, you want to know who is working for you. You also want your employees to know who they're working for. If there is no face to the person in the leadership position, there's no connection, no relationship, no empathy, no understanding, and no desire to give more than is asked, or paid for. Show up as a visible leader. Model a business of connected, real, and valuable people, accepting of others and willing to learn from everyone to make your own business better.

External

Showing up outside your business is imperative as well. Think about how many people you count on make your business work. Don't just show up when it is time to get your taxes done, know something about your accountant and make time to show up when your presence says, "I appreciate you," not just, "get this done." This is the same for your suppliers, your business peers, your networking partners, your joint venture and affiliate connections, and so on. In business, we need to be visible to people who support and share in our business with our prospects and clients.

I know that finding time to do the work is challenging enough, without me telling you that you also have to find time to go above and beyond. But it doesn't have to be painful. In fact, if it is painful, or too arduous, it is likely too extravagant. Small gestures that say, "I appreciate you" are often more than enough. Think about the last time you received something that was unexpected and appreciated. One time for me it was a simple text from a busy friend asking how my talk went. The fact that she took a few seconds out of her day to remember that I was away speaking, and that I had just likely finished my talk was impressive, as she has a busy law practice and a speaking career of her own. That one act spoke more to me of how much she cared than if she had sent flowers or a card.

Show up when people expect you, show up when they need you, and also show up when they don't need or expect you.

How to Show Up for Yourself

I remember when my oldest child was still in elementary school and a friend and I were chatting about kids and challenges. I was spending a lot of time looking for ways to help my kids socialize, exercise, engage, and become great human beings, but I was not looking after me.

I was run down, tired, unkempt, and it was showing up in my business (which was very new at the time). With her authority as a therapist, my friend turned to me and said, "Give yourself permission to look after you." It really hit home. I started to cry. It was like I had never realised I had the authority to give myself permission. My kids looked to me to show up and be the authority. My business expected me to show up and do what was needed to be done. I was looking after my family well and my business well, but I was neglecting me. What if something happened to me because of this? What if I became ill because I was not looking after me? Why was I not showing up for myself?

When we are new to our businesses it feels a lot like we have to give, give, give (or in business terms invest, invest, invest). We have to invest our time to make it work. We have to invest our money to have product, training, marketing, etc. We have to invest our hearts, or we won't do the work. And this is the same for your family, especially if you are a woman. For some reason, a large majority of women are hardwired to feel they are responsible for the overall wellbeing of the family. Nurture or nature, I don't know, but I see it a lot. Men, on the other hand, seem to have an easier time focusing on what has to get done to ensure they have what they need for their families. So, if your time, money, and heart are already invested in a new business and a family, where is the time for YOU?

My friend, a performance sales and leadership coach, is fond of saying, "There is no way to make time." This is his response to the common phrase, "we'll have to make time to..." and he is right. There is no extra time for you if you don't book that time. So, to show up for yourself you must ensure that YOU are in your calendar, that money for your health and wellbeing is set aside, and that you take time to be emotionally fulfilled. If you don't think this is possible, then I recommend you read Dr. Wayne W. Dyer's book "Excuses Begone!" You will definitely see how to overcome a life of excuse-making and do what it is you want to do and need to do.

Chapter 14 Never Stop Learning

> *No one gets stronger or wiser by winning. You get stronger and wiser in the preparation to win.*
> **Barb Stuhlemmer**

I am very happy to talk about my family's position on education and, at the same time, I am very sad to discuss the current situation of education.

When I was growing up I was told, over-and-over, that I could do anything I wanted to do. And I totally bought into the concept, both in terms of the opportunity to pick any path I wanted, and the realization I was smart enough to do whatever I wanted to do. When I hit about Grade 7 or 8, my parents were unable to assist me with any of my homework. The things I was learning were beyond their knowledge and that was OK with me. The older I got, the more I realized I was going to have to work hard to save enough money to afford post-secondary education. All of my father's sisters went to university, but his parents had not been university-educated, nor was my father. My mother's sisters went to university, as did her mother and her eight siblings, but my mother did not. My parents wanted something great for me that they had not accomplished for themselves. They raised me in an environment that saw learning and graduation as an important goal. The idea was to use my education to land a great job for my entire life.

An entire generation bought into the fallacy that you could live a full life on a single education. We saw the fall-out from this way of thinking when our country experienced huge manufacturing job losses; these were followed by losses in jobs that supported manufacturing: engineers, academics, scientists, writers, and other people who had spent tens of thousands of dollars on post-secondary education.

These people had purchased an education to obtain a higher-level job and were awfully surprised when their job and others like it moved to the countries that are now home to many of the manufacturing plants.

It has become quite clear that the days of being smart, finishing school, and getting a job for life ended several decades ago. Being smart isn't enough. Being educated isn't enough. We need to be adaptive and creative. We must be constantly learning new skills and mindsets. I would say this trait is important for great entrepreneurs and great employees. In the chapter on "It's All About You," I stated that your business must be filled with "intrapreneurs." These are people who work in a business to make a wage, of course, but also for the pride of seeing the business do well. They're often willing to work for a small piece of equity, or the potential for full ownership in the business. These are the employees with an entrepreneurial spirit and mind. The business is not theirs but they treat its success as their accomplishment.

If you want to be a great entrepreneur, stay on the path to greater knowledge and ensure everyone that can affect your product, client experience, or bottom-line has the same opportunity to learn.

Six Places to Grow Personally

I often find myself saying things like, "I've grown and changed *so much* these last few months!"

When I first started my business, I was like a cocky teen with a mindset to match. I was an adult with no experience in business but I was confident and knowledgeable enough to make competent judgement calls.

Thankfully, I am a constant learner. The more I learned, the more I needed to learn, and the more I grew and changed.

Here are six areas of learning opportunities for business owners:

1. Learn How to Communicate Better

As a technical writer and trainer with more than 20 years of experience, I am considered by many as an expert communicator. Recently I've taken to reading books on communication to better understand the nuances of human relationships. Here are three things you can do to improve your communication skills:

1. Read

Reading is a great way to learn how to interpret and use industry-specific communications and everyday language. Your opportunities to learn through reading include:

- Newspapers

- Online articles and blogs

- Books (Fiction and Non-fiction, "How to" books, Self-improvement books, etc.)

- Rules, directions, procedures, and recipes

2. Learn about Communications

Spend time learning more about human relationships, and verbal and non-verbal communication. There are hundreds of great books, courses, and programs in which you can invest. I paid for coaching certification, not because I wanted to be a coach or needed to know how to run a coaching business, but because I wanted to embrace the "best practices" tools and skills that a coach uses to support their clients. I've invested in other support systems that have given me different access to energetic communication and one of my next investments will be in training in the field of neurolinguistic programming (NLP).

Your own investment does not have to be this extensive, but do try to learn something about being a great communicator. It will make a difference to your business.

Below are three books I recommend to better understand communication and language.

- *What Every BODY is Saying [2008]* – by Joe Navarro and Marvin Karlins

- *Influence: The Psychology of Persuasion [2006]* - by Cialdini, Robert B., PhD

- *The Yes Factor - Get What You Want. Say What You Mean* [2011] by Tonya Reiman

You can also take courses in person or online, or follow people who are well-known and trusted for their leadership skills and their ability to connect with people on a deeper level.

I started out learning about marketing communications from masters like Lorrie Morgan-Ferrero, Seth Godin, and Fabienne Fredrickson. By following what they did, reading their blogs, and attending their events, I started the process of understanding the difference between technical writing and marketing writing. I started investing in programs with them and I coached directly under experts such as Fabienne, Sydni Craig-Hart, Lisa Sasevich, and Laura Gisborne.

Remember, some of our greatest mentors are people we may never actually get a chance to meet, but who have left us great inspiration through their words. Find the way that is easiest for you to learn and stay on top of it, always.

3. Write

When I started writing I hired an editor to review all of the technical manuals I created. We would spend an hour going over all the changes she felt needed to be made and she would give me pointers on how I could improve. Each time we did this, I made fewer mistakes.

When I started writing marketing documents, articles and blogs, I continued to have my writing reviewed.

The reviews not only give me feedback on the basics of grammar and spelling, but they also gave me insight into interpretation of meaning, how we connect ideas, and a variety of insights into how others might perceive my meaning. It has made me a better leader, and now when I have something to say I find my message is weighted with more trust because I deliver it more skillfully. Becoming a better writer has also made me a better speaker.

Saying what you mean, and ensuring that you are understood, accepted, and valued helps us gain influence. If you want to be more influential in your home, business, community and life, be a better, all-around communicator.

2. Improve How You Think (Psychology)

No one is going to be able to tell you what to think—no one, that is, other than you. Changing your mindset to improve your results will require you to look for new ways to think about the situation and people you find in your life. Try some of these options to start and maintain that shift:

- Take an improvisational (improv) theatre class
- Join an advisory board
- Read *Thinking Fast and Slow* [2013] by Daniel Kahneman
- Get a coaching certification
- Hire a coach
- Befriend a family-law lawyer or therapist
- Become a great listener
- Take yoga or learn to meditate.
- Join a weekly networking group
- Take a training course

Many things that I have experienced have affected my mindset in subtle yet profound ways and all I can say is that I am happier and more able to help people, my family, and myself because of the skills I have learned through experience.

3. Discern When to Delegate

Understanding varies in depth. We can fully understand the tiniest intricacy of an object or simply understand its general use. I've learned that it's not necessary to understand every aspect of every job within your business. I have written help systems and manuals for many software and hardware products and I have learned hundreds of proprietary software applications. Needless to say, I am an expert at learning tech. In my business, though, it simply becomes overwhelming to take on full knowledge of every application that I have to use. I can write HTML but I had an expert put together my website; I hired more experts to set up my membership site, tie in my shopping cart, and put together my newsletter template, and so on. Being an expert at learning tech does not make it fun or necessary for me to learn more tech in my business. If you are taking on every new application, setting up every new process, training in every new technique, etc. you will not have time to do what you do best in your business and your business will suffer.

Whenever I can get someone better than me to do work that will take me twice as long and end up overwhelming me, I hire them. It allows me to focus on what I am best at doing and thus helps my business grow.

4. Stay in Growth Mode

We might know the basics of business design, setup, operations, management, and finance...but there are hundreds of other ways for us to make more money, work less, and create more business. A business owner must always be in growth mode to remain competitive and relevant.

I once worked for a small company that had 23 employees and had been in business for more than 25 years. They had clients around the world and they were one of the few businesses that could do what they did. They were unique and relevant. As technology started to change more rapidly every year, they quickly found that they could not keep up with new ideas.

They could develop new ideas, and they were smart enough to bring them to life, but they had never had to be in growth mode before. Like a teen who had never learned to study, they were in full catch-up mode behind their competitors.

Always be growing, because if you are not growing, you are in decline. If not now, then soon. Try something new at least once a week.

- Look for new opportunities
- Take a new path to or from your place of work
- Do something differently
- Ask for input and feedback
- Meet new people
- Go somewhere new to you
- Eat new foods (try a different restaurant or recipe)
- Speak publicly
- Debate a topic

5. Learn about Yourself

If you are not dead, then you are not finished. Keep growing personally. Keep pushing to be a better person. Keep looking for ways to feel more accomplished. Keep stretching into new areas. Don't just add new skills, also add new abilities, mindsets, and areas of focus. Celebrate all your milestones.

Be totally aware that you are the artist, with many paintings; some are masterpieces, many are practice or trial pieces, and some are unfinished works of art. All have the touch of your unique perspective that is driven by your life experiences and learnings.

One of my favourite exercises is to write out my accomplishments. The first time I tried to make a list of 100 accomplishments it took me weeks. I got to about #55 and then I had to stop. To continue I had to reach back in time: to my 30s, my 20s, my teens, my childhood. I wrote down everything I had ever done that I felt was an accomplishment. I finished the list and that in itself was a huge accomplishment!

It doesn't end with #100 unless that is where your life ends. Your list of accomplishments is a living document. I add large accomplishments when they happen and then every year on my birthday I write another 100. It gets easier every year because I continue to learn and grow, and with that comes new opportunities and experiences, all of which involve some level of accomplishment.

Note – this list is for you. You never have to show anyone else, so be generous and capture everything you have done that you feel is an accomplishment in your life.

6. Work on Becoming a Great Leader

I truly believe that this is one of the key entrepreneurial skills to master. I don't want to talk much about this as I highly recommend reading and learning from John C. Maxwell. His teachings on this subject are extensive. My favourite book of his on this subject is *The 5 levels of Leadership*.

What I found as I became a better leader was that more work gets done, fewer errors are made, and more people become happier. Tell me, who doesn't want a business full of happy, efficient, and accurate workers?

Failing Your Way to Success

And, finally, in terms of learning, I believe in the saying, "fail early and fail fast."

I talked about a fail-fast system earlier in the chapter on "Running Out of Money." Failure is such a negative word. It simply means you have learned something about marketing, your business, process, your client, yourself, or others, that you will be able to apply to the next project, business, product, etc.

If you go through life never failing, you likely have not taken enough risk. Business growth and success without risk is not possible if you truly want to be entrepreneur.

As an example, I watched a 72-year-old man make a pitch once on the Canadian show "Dragons' Den" (similar to the USA show "Shark Tank"). This man had invested everything he owned in his business: his house, farm, and savings of close to $1,000,000. He had sold only about $180,000 of his product over his 15 years of business. When asked why he had not closed his business years earlier, he responded, "I am not a quitter" and "I have never failed at anything."

Arlene Dickenson, one of the show's "Dragons", was actually moved to tears by the innocence of this massive loss. He had already failed and he did not know it. He had lost everything, and yet he arrogantly kept on believing that if he kept trying it would mean that he had lost nothing. The only thing he really had was an unrealistic belief that he had never failed.

If he had recognized the failure years ago, when he still had money and time to invest, he might have been able to do something great. He definitely would have learned something about business and himself.

"I encourage you to use your passion to create a desire to do something. Use this desire to accomplish your goals. Use your goals to fulfill your purpose. Make sure your business aligns with your purpose and you will more easily find your entrepreneurial success."

- **Barb Stuhlemmer**

Chapter 15 Find Your Passion/Purpose

> *The starting point of all achievement is* DESIRE. *Keep this constantly in mind. Weak* desire *brings weak results.*
> **Napoleon Hill**

Without desire, there is no motivation to make something happen that we actually want to happen.

We can certainly create a mess in our lives by doing things without intent. For example, look at the social rates of teen pregnancy, debt, obesity, addiction, etc. These happen because of a lack of passion, purpose, and desire, amongst other factors.

Think about a time when you really wanted something: a new car, a house, new shoes. Even if you initially thought you could not afford it, if your desire was great enough, you were able to find a way.

The key to achievement lies in the passion of your desire. If you are doing something you are passionate about, you will be able to stay motivated through the tough times. Your passion will ensure that you see it through and the achievement will fulfil your purpose in life, giving you a feeling of worth. We all want to feel that what we do matters. We want to feel that we add value and that we belong. Doing the work that we love that is aligned with our passion and purpose helps us stay motivated and adds value to our lives.

I knew what I was good at and what I liked doing, but it wasn't until I was in my forties that I really understood my purpose. Without a purpose, my desire was fragmented.

I would work at one thing, accomplish my goals, and then move on to something else. I was never fulfilled.

Before I understood how I fit into my world, I felt I was forcing my gifts on others.

I have to tell you that finding this path was not easy and outside assistance was instrumental in releasing me from my doubt, helping me to express my gifts, and empowering me to move forward.

One of my greatest experiences was to work with Nadia Tumas, the Life Purpose Decoder[13]. Her reading of who I am and what I do revealed the language I could use to describe my passion to help great people live their purpose to the fullest.

I encourage you to use your passion to create a desire to do something. Use this desire to accomplish your goals. Use your goals to fulfill your purpose.

Make sure your business aligns with your purpose and you will more easily find your entrepreneurial success.

Check-in

Find the people who can see you for who you are, free you from the singular perspective of who you can become, and empower you to do your work every day with gratitude. This will allow you to feel purposeful in all you do.

If you have not done so yet, go back to the chapter on "The Basics" and complete the desire exercise that I recommended.

---

[13] http://www.nadiatumas.com/

Chapter 16: Keeping Secrets

> *To keep your own secrets is wisdom; but to expect others to keep them is folly.*
> **William Scott Downey,** Author of 'Proverbs'

This chapter is on keeping secrets. After all, not everything you know should be shared with every person you know. The question to answer is, "When do I talk, and to whom?"

One of my first lessons in secrecy came as a teen. I hung around with several girlfriends. We did everything together but not always as a group. Two here… three there… we mixed and matched, depending on the event and the people, or the destination. I remember telling one friend, in confidence, something about another friend. After all, we were close friends. The problem was, so were she and the girlfriend about whom the gossip revolved. Something that should not have been said now required an apology and penance. We are still friends today, thanks to my friend's graciousness, but things could have gone differently if she had chosen to not forgive me.

In business, information that does not further the growth of your people and their efforts for the company is likely not information they need to know. As an owner, if you tell something to one person in your business, you must expect that information could be shared with everyone in your business, as each person is likely friends with someone else. For many in your business, it will be tough for them to hear challenges about you or the business, especially when they neither have the answer nor the ability to make it better. For example, if, as an employee, you are privy to all the finances you may not understand why investments are being made.

Why is money being spent when times are tough? Think about an opportunity you may have had in your business already. One that required you to invest more money in growth, a new product, a trial, training, etc. As the owner, you are thinking about the outcome – the big picture results – the bottom line. As an employee you may be thinking, "if this doesn't work, will there be enough to pay me?" It is more difficult to see the connection between the risk of the money going out and the wage you expect to receive at the end of your pay period.

You are the business owner taking the risks and likely the only one to be on the line to lose much more than just a job if things don't go well. You will be required to invest in yourself for training and image-boosters (like clothes) that others may see as vain or extravagant. But if getting training increases your ROI, for example, then it is important.

There are people who need to know what you are doing. People, like your accountant, who can help you evaluate your expenses to ensure they represent the right investments.

I'm required to travel a lot in order to connect with peers who are doing what I want to implement in my own business. I've invested in a lot of high-end training with people who are more successful than I am.

But if I had told some of my closest friends or family members at that time that I was investing thousands of dollars to travel and get training when I was struggling to get the sales started in the business, they would have suggested that I should think about just getting a job.

By keeping that knowledge to myself, I allow the people who have a lot of fear around failure, and no risk tolerance or business insight, to be free from the worry that comes with the knowledge. The people who understand and can help will not react the same way.

Choosing to let only the right people in to your inner circle ensures that you take into account only legitimate insights from people with the right kind of experience. It will save you time, money, and anxiety and allow you to be more confident and, ultimately, more successful.

In the words of Napoleon Hill, "Take no one into your confidence, except the members of your mastermind group. [Those people] who will be in complete sympathy and harmony with your purpose."

Deciding by Vote - Three Mindsets

When you ask for someone's advice on something you expect that they have some knowledge or understanding to be able to give their insight. Asking for someone's view when they cannot see the landscape of the issue is counterproductive. Their answers are just guesses and that is worse than a bad point of view. Perspective without a view can hamper good judgement and stop growth.

When you are the one at the top making decisions, you are pretty much on your own when it comes to the final say and the responsibility of risk.

So, who do you talk to when your ideas need vetting, challenges need strategy with insight, or problems need compassion with the understanding of experience? Who do you turn to when you need advice based on empathy, and personal expertise that is not based on fear?

If you are making decisions in your company by getting a vote from all your employees, your decisions may often not meet the business's needs: it is not possible to share all information about all business secrets, so your voters will not have the information they need to make great decisions. They will have a perspective without a view. So, who has a vote?

There are three types of mindsets that you might have as owner of your business and below is a diagram that shows the decision path these three mindsets follow. Descriptions of each mindset follow the diagram.

Job/Employee	Other (e.g. equity partner)	Owner
Get the job ↓ Do the work ↓ Collect the pay ↓ Spend money	Hire with buy-in ↓ Invest time for growth ↓ Do the Work ↓ Reap the benefits or fall with the business	Market the product/service ↓ Sell the product/service ↓ Do the work ↓ Invoice ↓ Spend/Invest the money/pay out/pay self

Employee Mindset

As you can see in the first column of the three mindsets, the Employee has a job. They are expected to produce a specific level of work, and collect a pay cheque that they will spend. They are part of the operation of the business. They are not expected to make business decisions. They do want to see the business continue so they can continue to collect a wage. Their perspective on growth is that if the business does better, they may get a raise. If the business fails, it is not their responsibility or their fault.

Other Mindset

This mindset may belong to a commission-based employee who may also own a small percentage of the business; it can also be an advisory board member or mentor who receives dividends.

Or it can be a non-voting partner. They're not expected to make business decisions but may have exceptional vision for the growth of the business, and their input is expected.

This person has "buy-in": they have more to lose in the outcome of decisions made. Great decisions will ensure they get their commission or dividend. A bad decision may cost them more than their job, and result in a failure that's attributed to them.

Owner Mindset
As the owner, you will be focused on the bottom line. Can you make enough to pay wages, invest in the company, and hopefully make money yourself? There are more parts of the business to consider when a decision is to be made and it is less focused on one individual's outcome. Getting to the right decision will affect the entire company and the customers.

Side-bar

For healthy business growth, it is important that you understand I am not condoning keeping your employees in the dark. The more ideas and goals you can get your team involved with, the more they can take ownership of their contribution, and the more they are on board with your direction.

There is a fine line between getting your people to support and contribute to the company goals and the over-sharing of personal issues that would burden them in their position. Your employees are not your personal HR department. You do not get to vet your issues to them.

Your employees should know the big picture (whether it is good or bad). Their insights into how their efforts can add to or hamper a plan is important. Understanding your connections to other businesses, your personal struggle, tax issues, or other details of running the business that is outside their core expertise is not the best use of their time. Use your experts for their expertise.

As an owner, you will see the outcome of decisions differently from anyone else in the business.

When I look for a confidant with whom I can air my concerns, review a decision, strategize a difficult plan, etc., I look for someone who has done the work for themselves and can both empathize with my position and give expert insight without emotion. I look outside my business for that person.

Below is a list of all the different types of people I have used to talk through ideas, build plans, and share failures with over the years.

Who Are They?
Mentors (Past bosses and friends who are or were business owners)
Coaches (Entrepreneurs who were successfully running their own businesses)
Peers (Others running a business)
Competitors (Others doing what I'm doing)
Suppliers (People from whom I would buy services)
Contractors (People who contract in my industry)
Friends (Who run businesses)
Family (For very specific conversations)
Teachers (Those I pay to learn from)
Advisory Board (I set this up for my first business)
Mastermind Group (peers in a structured, regular meeting for support)

Asking your employees to put their fear aside and take a leap to make a decision that will cost the company money in hopes of making more money, is asking for more than you likely hired them for. They are not in a job to risk their home life, they want security and a regular paycheque. Having your own board of experts will create a different result. The expert on the board is hired to bring insights that will help grow the company.

It is not their core income, nor will it affect their financial stability if they do not have the position. In fact, being a mentor or board member can often be a volunteer position. When an idea is offered by the board, all aspects are investigated and there is no "fear for self" that will be in conflict with their judgment. Their best reward is to see the company succeed as it will add to their accomplishments.

If you want a decision to be effective for your company, the decisions cannot be fear-based, not by employees and not by you. As the leader, confident decision-making will need to be one of your strongest core skills. As Darren Hardy has discovered and discusses in his book, *The Entrepreneurial Rollercoaster*, businesses don't fail for the reasons most think, they fail for internal reasons, like fear. Find yourself a team of people you can call on to help you make the best decisions for your company, and lead with confidence. It will be the best thing you can do for the growth you wish to create.

Other Sharing

The gossip story I shared earlier had minimal repercussions. In business, the smallest thing you share can cost you hundreds or thousands of dollars, even when you choose your words wisely. Not everyone listens, interprets intentions, or remembers details the same way. If you are making a suggestion to lead to a deal or a sale, you will need to put it into a contract to ensure it is understood. If that information should not be shared, like the sale of shares, distribution channels, patent information etc., then your contract should include a non-disclosure agreement section.

I have had clients who hired contractors and then gave them access to their customers. They then lost their customers to the contractor because their contract did not have a non-compete clause.

Sharing important business information should always be viewed as valued property of the company. One wrong word could mean you can't collect on a final payment, may require you to "eat the cost" of some service or purchase, give away your time for free, or require a refund you cannot afford. When you are the boss, the money you have invested, the time you have spent, and the risks you have endured earn you the right to keep some of the business information protected and secret.

So, how do you have a progressive company with an open-leadership paradigm that requires a flat management structure while you hold all the secrets? The answer is "you don't." Well, not completely, anyway.

To ensure business secrecy, while keeping an open line of communication, you need greater buy-in. The best way to help people feel they have "skin-in-the-game" is to give them ownership. If you are a small company, as the key person in the business you will create a team interested in seeing their piece grow. Not just for money, but also for the reward of seeing their efforts create something of value. The challenge is that if they did not pay for that right to own (with time or money) they will not be invested and will not be as willing to take the risk needed to make the scary decisions. They will "vote with fear" and you will be challenged again with sharing secrets that can affect the business growth and the corporate bottom line.

Unlike most others in your company, as the business owner, you get the vote and you should know all the details.

Starbucks employees all own shares in the company. They know a lot about the corporate growth model, direction, and plans, but they were not consulted for strategies to overcome their failing business back in the 90s. Asking thousands of people who are all worried about their jobs to make some tough decisions about building, investing, cutting costs, and closing stores would not have benefited Starbucks in that tough time.

Starbucks needed strong, dedicated employees who served their customers with the same, high-level customer service people were used to, and they would not have done that if everyone was worried about the vote they were expected to make about closing stores.

What I'm saying is that you cannot hire a Sherpa to lead you up a mountain if they have not been there themselves and they are not a mountain climber. The people who lead you up the mountain of entrepreneurship must know the way, understand the risks, and understand the dangers of this climb, while helping ensure your safety as much as they can.

Wrap-up (Part III)

When you started reading this section of the book you had already put the foundation for your business in place and you had set goals to create a bigger business and be the person who makes the hard decisions. Part III of this book covered the key to being an awakened entrepreneur, which is all about living it every day.

Make this transformation permanent by knowing exactly what your next few years will hold in store for you. Do the work of identifying all the different roles in your business and challenge yourself to be limited to the three roles that align with your passion.

To let go of the responsibilities that do not match your top three roles, start by identifying the three roles you absolutely hate to do. Put them on your "dislike list."

Set a goal in your business plan to offload each of these three roles over time. As you get rid of one role you dislike, add another to your "dislike list." Continue doing this until all you are left with are your three favourite roles. When you are only responsible for the three roles you love, you will be doing the work of your passion.

If these three favourite positions align with your purpose, as well, then you have arrived at the goal of this book, which is to be awake in your work within your business.

If these three positions do not align with your purpose, then determine whether or not you should be in this business at all. To be fully awake you need to be doing the work that fully aligns with your purpose, desire, and aspirations.

Finally

The journey from employee to entrepreneur is akin to the journey from childhood to adult. At each point along the path you can be the best at what you do — better than you were in the past, and even better than your peers—but you can still know very little about many of the things that come with experience and maturity.

Spend a great deal of time learning about business and not just doing the work. Even if you cannot see it in yourself, accept that you will not likely have an entrepreneurial mindset during your first year in business. Truly, that first year is all about grasping the fundamentals of running the business, figuring out that you are "The One" who does all the work, gets the prospects, makes the sales, creates the plans, invests the time and money, makes the mistakes, and takes all the responsibility.

There is a lot to learn about business that has little to do with the entrepreneurial mindset, yet it all leads to the growth required to step into that paradigm.

As you start understanding the day-to-day aspects of running your business, more opportunity will start coming into view. The employee will think "I can't" and the entrepreneur will think "How can I?" If opportunity is followed by an excuse not to act, then you are not there yet. Opportunity must be followed by action to investigate the options.

When you're ready and working in this mindset you will invest in risk and be willing to step into "scary" decision-making.

Don't be like the business owner I talked about in the "Decision-Making" chapter. She had been working for 17 years and still could not create the business she wanted. It was a constant struggle. When an opportunity came to make a significant change that would increase her business and allow her to take on more clients, she turned it down because she could not make the decision. Her decisions were made in fear, without true insight for a growth plan and without valuing her company, her clients, or herself. She worried more about what her husband would think about her than what she should think about her business.

Remember, this is not your life, it is your business. If it is not working, close it down and start again with a different idea. Business should be treated like an investment and it needs to make money.

Once your business is running successfully, with systems and procedures, employees and processes, your time can be managed and your value can be calculated. The business could continue to run and grow under your leadership or you can sell it and start again... or not. Because once you have the entrepreneurial mindset, there is no going back. You cannot unlearn what you have learned. You will implement it and live it in everything you do.

I have often heard (and I've said this myself), "I feel completely unemployable." The person saying this does not feel incompetent. They are entrepreneurs and they don't think like employees any longer. They want more freedom to envision greater options that they can birth, grow and celebrate.

Entrepreneurs are not born, they are awakened from within the slumbering employee and, once released, they yearn to be the designer of something new and great. If that is where you are in life, I wish you all the best with your journey.

The journey from employee to entrepreneur is akin to the journey from childhood to adult. At each point along the path you can be the best at what you do — better than you were in the past, and even better than your peers—but you can still know very little about many of the things that come with experience and maturity. Spend a great deal of time learning about business and not just doing the work. Even if you cannot see it in yourself, accept that you will not likely have an entrepreneurial mindset during your first year in business. Truly, that first year is all about grasping the fundamentals of running the business, figuring out that you are "The One" who does all the work, gets the prospects, makes the sales, creates the plans, invests the time and money, makes the mistakes, and takes all the responsibility. There is a lot to learn about business that has little to do with the entrepreneurial mindset, yet it all leads to the growth required to step into that paradigm.

- Barb Stuhlemmer

Chapter 17 Tools and Resources

> *I have a low tolerance for people who complain about things but never do anything to change them. This led me to conclude that the single largest pool of untapped natural resources in this world is human good intentions that are never translated into actions.*
> **- Cindy Gallop (BrainyQuote.com)**

Now that you have an understanding of what it takes to "Do" business, to learn how to build and run a business, to implement and grow your business, and to live a life where your business fully supports you, you now have the path to become a powerful entrepreneur.

Take your good intentions about doing the work in this book and put them into action.

Tap your natural resource of good intentions to make a business that will support you until you are ready to move on, and not because you have run out of money, but because you want to.

You can do this. You can have a life that allows you to make good money doing what you love to do. Do the work that allows you to play.

Here are some extra resources and tools from the stories throughout the book to help you really make your strategic planning and review concrete and doable.

Five Books Every Entrepreneur Should Read

Never stop learning – and never stop reading. Some of my favourite mentors I only know through their books. Below are five books that had a significant impact on the direction of my business and the solidification of my entrepreneurial mindset.

The E-Myth Mastery (Michael E. Gerber)
This is for business owners who understand what it takes to "Do" their business and who want to see what it takes to "Be" their business. It is about management of the growing business. This book is the third in a series of four about the E-Myth (Entrepreneurial Myth) that Mr. Gerber has developed.

Lynchpin (Seth Godin)
This book gave me a great understanding of how my uniqueness plays a powerful role in the value I offer my clients. It is also a very good book for employees who want to be indispensable in their jobs.

The 5 Levels of Leadership (John C. Maxwell)
I have listened to this audiobook three times. I found the insights into where I am and what I'm missing as a leader have been invaluable both as a strong leader in my business and when helping others inspire their teams to step up to greatness as well. A leader of leaders is not a small aspiration, and this book is a must-read for anyone with that desire.

Blink: The Power of Thinking Without Thinking and Outliers: The Story of Success (Malcolm Gladwell)
I love books that are based on research. Both of these books provide information that helps a business owner become a stronger person and understand how their business, and they themselves, act and react to situations, trends, and life events— and how trends and life events result from the actions people take.

Good To Great (Jim Collins)
Having an understanding of what a great company looks like, and what makes it significantly better than a "good" company, was eye opening to me. Again, this is a book based on research that really answers a lot of questions around if, and why, certain things should be done in a business, and how they affect the bottom line.

Other Books Mentioned (Available on Indigo or Amazon)

- *Excuses Begone!: How to Change Lifelong, Self-Defeating Thinking Habits* by Dr. Wayne W. Dyer

- *Think and Grow Rich by Napoleon Hill* (I own an audio, a PDF and a gold-edged premium edition of this book – worth it!)

- *What Every BODY is Saying: An Ex-FBI Agent's Guide to Speed-Reading People* – by Jo Navarro & Marvin Karlins

- *Thinking Fast and Slow* by Daniel Kahneman

- *Influence: The Psychology of Persuasion* by Robert B. Cialdini

- *The Yes Factor: Get What You Want. Say What You Mean* by Tanya Reiman

- See last page for additional book resources.

In addition, a textbook that I use in the college where I teach is *Small Business: An Entrepreneur's Plan* by Ron Knowles & Chris Castillo. It is a great resource for creating a plan to start and run a business.

Desire Statement
Desire + Passion + Intent + Persistence = Success

> From Napoleon Hill's book, **Think and Grow Rich**:
> "Desire is the starting point of all achievement"

What is your desire to accomplish? Not a wish, your dominating desire? If you desire it you can accomplish it!

What Motivates Me to Develop and Build This Company?

Read the chapter on Desire in Napoleon Hill's *Think and Grow Rich*. I recommend that you read this entire book, but if you cannot do that, then start by reading this one chapter. Before you do the work of creating your desire statement go back to the chapter on the Desire Statement in this book, specifically the part that describes "The Pitfall" of this exercise so you will get it right. If you have not done so yet I've provided a FREE PDF version of his book. Get your free copy of Think and Grow Rich:

http://www.theentrepreneurawakening.com/courses/the-entrepreneur-awakening-book

Method
The method by which DESIRE for success can be transformed into your reality is defined in the six steps starting on page 24 of Napoleon Hill's book.

1. "Be definite as to the amount." More specifically, be definite to the outcome of your desire. (The actual desire – e.g. "...my son would hear and speak.")

2. Determine exactly what you intend to give.

3. Establish a definite date.

4. Create a definite plan

5. Write out a clear, concise statement

6. Read your written statement aloud, twice daily.

Using the table below, the structured statement described in Napoleon Hill's book, and the distinctions pointed out in the chapter on "The Basics", create your desire statement. You can also download a PDF of this statement from my website[BS1]

Be definite as to the outcome you desire	I desire to...
Determine exactly what you intend to give	In return I will...
Establish a definite date	By the first day of...
Create a definite plan	... I will follow this plan...
Write out a clear statement of belief	I believe I will have this...

HeartMath

Look up Heart Math online or use this link to get more answers:

http://www.heartmath.org/faqs/heartmath-system/heartmath-system-faqs.html

SWOT Analysis: Below is a template you can use to perform a SWOT analysis on yourself, your business and your rivals. Do one table for each and include it in your business plan. I've included an example for each field to help get you started:

Strengths	Weaknesses	Opportunities	Threats						
e.g. I personally know the director of my largest potential client	e.g. I do not have credentials to bring me instant credibility	e.g. The regulations are changing and more people are going to have to pay for my type of services	e.g. If I get sick I do not have someone to take over my work and my clients may suffer						

Website Information

Domain Names
This book's Information may not be valid for long. Technology changes so quickly it's hard to create an up-to-date resource. So, I will simply suggest that you ask your web designer, another business owner, your local Chamber of Commerce, or other local business resources where they go to purchase domain names. The company I use (GoDaddy.com) is easy to work with and they have exceptional customer support. I never try to buy my domain online. I always call and they walk me through what I need and always make it as simple for me as possible.

Browsers
Again, this often is preference-based. Mozilla, which developed and manages Firefox, is one of the most commonly-used browsers available. The good thing about something being so heavily used is that they get a lot of feedback for improvements, there are a lot of third party applications and widgets, and they likely have a larger budget to manage their software then a smaller, lesser known browser. Microsoft Internet Explorer, Google Chrome, and Apple's Safari are three other heavily used browsers. Most applications and online operations are tested in these four browsers.

The mobile device market is quickly replacing computer based operations and must also be evaluated. In 2014, for the first time, online browsing from a mobile device eclipsed computer-originated browsing. The sales of mobile devices are still on a steep incline, whereas the sale of computers is declining.

[Source KCPG http://www.smartinsights.com/digital-marketing-strategy/internet-trends-2014-mary-meeker/ - @KPCB via Morgan Stanley Research 2013]

Your Downloads
FREE PDF version of Napoleon Hill's book, *Think and Grow Rich*
Desire Statement Table / SWOT Analysis Template
Website: www.bit.ly/EntrepreneurAwakeningFreeResources

About The Author:

As a Speaker, Author, TV Show Host, College Instructor, and Chair of the Advisory board for The School of Entrepreneurship, Barb Stuhlemmer is a Master Business Strategist who works to strengthen the courage of 6-figure business owners to take extraordinary action.

Barb Stuhlemmer elevates the belief system of successful entrepreneurs to ensure they reach their biggest goals that will change their life and often the world.

She has been in the medical device and software industries for over 20 years. She has worked in small business most of her life and now she owns two businesses of her own.

Barb Stuhlemmer notes: "We all deserve to experience the creativity of envisioning a business and seeing that business successfully implemented and profitable."

Entrepreneur Awakening is Barb Stuhlemmer's first published book and is already drawing widespread interest from those seeking expert entrepreneurial advice.

She can be reached at barb@blitzbusinesssuccess.com

Manor House
905-648-2193